Pythiism

Of related interest:

My Autistic Awakening: Unlocking the potential for a life well lived

myautisticawakening.com

Contemplative Therapy for Clients on the Autism Spectrum: A Reflective Integration Therapy manual for psychotherapists and counsellors

rlharrispsy.com/RIT

RIT For Kids: Contemplative therapy for young children on the autism spectrum (ages 5–12)

ritforkids.com

Pythiism

Reframing autism as an alternative form of consciousness

RACHAEL LEE HARRIS

FOREWORD BY BARB COOK

pythiism.com

First published in 2021
by Rachael Lee Harris
PO BOX 385
Burpengary QLD 4505
Australia

rlharrispsy.com
rlharrispsy@gmail.com

ISBN 978-0-6485344-1-9

Printed and bound in Australia

 A catalogue record for this
book is available from the
National Library of Australia

*Those on the autism spectrum have unprecedented access to the
unconscious – being seated within it.*

pythism

a revolutionary theory of autism

Contents

About Pythiism

"An alternative form of consciousness distinguished as an oscillation of psychic energy between the unconscious and conscious mind informing one's whole field of perception: cognitive, emotional, social, physical and spiritual"

Pythiism: Reframing Autism as an Alternative Form of Consciousness – the first new major theory of autism since 1944

Asserts that autism is based, not in the brain, but in the psyche: where mind interfaces with matter – a seismic shift in focus from empirical to intuitive observation.

Re-examines not only the established major symptoms of autism, but also includes rarely or never covered areas of autism research: a psycho-evolutionary perspective, the existential emotions, and psychic phenomena and spirituality – finally solving the anomalies of autism that scientific reductionism is unable to reach.

Opens a conversation with academics, mental health professionals and most importantly people on the autism spectrum: presenting not only an equally valid point of reference for understanding themselves, but also a better one, revealing an alternative form of human consciousness hidden in plain sight.

Tells the Story of Pythia, providing an archetype and template for autism that informs the narrative throughout, drawing parallels between autistic presentation and that of the Oracle of Delphi.

Foreword

I've always been a deep thinker from a young age, a philosopher of existence, pondering life's mysteries, both in the material and spiritual realms. I've often felt like I didn't belong in the time in which I was born. In fact, many people on the autism spectrum feel a sense of not belonging to this age, but to that of the past.

Those of us on the spectrum are often driven by intense emotions and empathy for people past and present, the world around us, for the environment, and the animals that reside alongside us. But our fellow humans that think differently to us, who live in the conscious realm, miss the true beauty of being in synergy with the unconscious and conscious mind.

The parts of the Pythian mind, conscious and unconscious, work together in harmony to create our very own experience of what we perceive of the world, with the unconscious allowing us to have a foot in both realms.

Scientists have barely scratched the surface of understanding the dynamics and depth of how our minds work. They are slowly recognising that there is something far more than just connections, transactions and actions of a physical and medicalised existence.

Within this very book, Rachael delves into the mind, retracing the human experience back to its beginnings to give a unique perspective of how we, on the spectrum, are more than just a physical entity, a vessel to be pathologised. This thought-provoking book will be a catalyst in exploring the workings of the autistic mind and how the levels of consciousness play a critical role in what we perceive and understand.

It is high time that we explore these existential realities. As an autistic person and a philosophical thinker, with a thirst for knowledge that at times seems unquenchable, the words within this book ignite in me a passion to explore inwardly. For within ourselves lie the answers that each of us on the spectrum can truly seek and find: the recognition that our outward experience is a reflection of the internal self. It is time to turn down the noise and to listen, not just to me, but we.

Barb Cook
Editor and co-author, *Spectrum Women: Walking to the Beat of Autism*

Introduction

At the turn of the 20th century, when studying the nature of the human mind, the effects of the unconscious upon conscious thought were the talk of the academic world across Europe and North America. In conversation, academic papers and argument, the importance of comprehending how these two realms interfaced was self-evident. To understand the nature of the psyche, the combined processes of the unconscious and conscious mind, was to unlock no less than the secrets of the human condition.

At the forefront of this wild academic frontier were two great figures: Sigmund Freud and Carl Jung. Their interrogations into the nature of the unconscious had them collaborating closely for some years, before they eventually parted company over fundamental disagreements. Freud regarded the unconscious as the repository of repressed emotions and desires, whilst Jung regarded the unconscious as the storehouse of memories and experiences inherited from our ancestors. Freud believed that libido alone was responsible for the formation of the core personality, whereas Jung believed that the core traits of personal development were influenced by factors other than sexuality. This was a position from which their friendship never recovered.

The divorce between Freud and Jung may seem far removed from our current subject of autism, but what history teaches us is that Freud's theories, for much of the first half of the 20th century, received the lion's share of attention, strongly influencing the narrative of autism, as evidenced in Leo Kanner's 1943 paper entitled "Autistic Disturbances of Affective Contact", whose assertion of autism being caused by "Refrigerator Mothers" placed the blame on parents for withholding their affection from their children – parents whose own reserve seemed to neatly fit this theory. Even today in France, a Freudian psychoanalytical approach remains the theory of choice for a majority of therapists who continue to regard autism as an expression of negative unconscious feelings of children towards their mother, many of whom remain hidden away in psychiatric facilities and hospitals throughout the country.

Despite this last bastion of Freudian thinking, "autism as pathology" continues to hold sway within psychological considerations, having been embedded within the *Diagnostic and Statistical Manual of Mental Disorders*, fifth edition (DSM-5) 2013 as Autism Spectrum Disorder (ASD). Its diagnostic criteria, couched in the negative terminology of lacks and deficits, of difficulties and restrictions, continues to echo Freud's pathological distrust of the unconscious, bearing out biases inherited from the pen of Freud himself.

The presentation known as "autism" isn't *business as usual*, by any means. By dint of its oddity, its very strangeness, it demands a fresh framework of enquiry, an intuitive lens to bring our assumptions about autism into sharp relief, one capable of interpreting autism from a standpoint of health rather than pathology, and that lens is found in the works of Carl Jung, namely, his theory of the unconscious.

Jung regarded the nature of consciousness in three-tiered form: the conscious, the personal unconscious and the collective unconscious. And it was this vision of the structure and dynamics of the human psyche that became the framework for all his scientific endeavours, making the interpretation of its processes and its psychological, physical and spiritual implications, the subject of his life's work.

Jung's writings regarding the unconscious mind were many, so I have endeavoured to condense his thought on this subject into a framework that encapsulates what is necessary for the purposes of understanding the concepts to be explored throughout this book.

The *conscious* is comprised of an awakened state of awareness that rises daily out of the depths of sleep, welling up from the primordial depths of an unconscious condition to apprehend the everyday.

The *personal unconscious* encompasses the sum of everything we have encountered in our personal lived experience: the myriad sensory experiences that have bypassed conscious thought, all those things remembered and hoped for, the joys recalled and the sorrows repressed, and all those future things quietly taking shape below the level of conscious thought, waiting to emerge into awareness in their own time.

The *collective unconscious* is of a different order again, encompassing the memories and experiences not individually acquired, but rather, collectively inherited from our ancestors, including those instincts within the human condition that are universally experienced regardless of culture and conditioning. Although theoretically, there is no limit to the depths of the unconscious, the layers of the psyche descend further and further into the darkness of the unknown, and materially speaking, are extinguished in the biological components of which all matter is comprised.

Jung, arguably the greatest contributor in modern times to our understanding of the human psyche, owed his capacity to harness the hidden nature of consciousness and to marshal its processes and relationships into distinct categories, in large part due to he himself being on the autism spectrum. His *inner experiences,* including his dreams and visions, informed his scientific work.

What Jung was not privy to, was that the relationship between the conscious and unconscious mind could exist in an alternative form, a form which he himself personally experienced, but nevertheless remained unaware of. What the nature of consciousness tells us, is that there are forms of knowledge that cannot be forced into conscious awareness, or indeed *through* conscious awareness, but rise at their own hour, and in their own time from the depths of the unconscious itself.

The present work, is such a revelation, and constitutes the first major new theory of autism to be posited since Leo Kanner and Hans Asperger's theories of autism were first published in 1943 and 1944, respectively. We stand at a juncture in time in which our understanding of autism, having for many decades taken up almost exclusive residence in terms of genetic and neurological considerations, is about to rediscover the role the unconscious plays in a whole population whose alternative form of consciousness has remained hidden for over one-hundred years in plain sight, and whose way of being in the world is defined by the author in the following way:

Pythiism (pronounced *pie-thi-ism*), also known as autism, is an alternative form of consciousness, distinguished as an oscillation of psychic energy between the unconscious and conscious mind informing one's whole field of perception: cognitive, emotional, social, physical and spiritual. In essence, Pythiism is best described as personhood seated in the unconscious whose psychic energy constantly moves between an unconscious and conscious state of being.

One morning in March 2016, I sat out in my garden pondering my life as a person on the autism spectrum, and my earliest years, as a child, often unreachable, *drawn into* my inner-world of fragmented images and fleeting emotions or *drawn out* by some subject of interest that had caught my attention, before *descending once more* into my inner-world, which caused my Year One teacher to remark to my mother, "Rachael is here physically, but that is all."

As I sat there considering these two seemingly opposite states of mind, in my mind's eye I suddenly saw a thin unbroken line rising and falling steadily between the two points, linking and connecting each in a harmonious wave form, and my mind supplied the answer: *What you are looking at is an oscillation between your unconscious and conscious mind. Your perception is moving between both.*

As spontaneously as this concept seemed to appear, I now see that this understanding had been stirring below the level of my own consciousness over many years, heralded by odd flashes of insight in my clinical work as a therapist treating clients on the autism spectrum, and, as on this occasion, manifested in reflections on my own life experience as a person on the autism spectrum.

From the moment this understanding of autism as an oscillation of psychic energy moving between the unconscious and conscious mind presented itself to me, I knew in an instant that I was duty bound to present it to others, and so I set myself to doing so, submitting to the process of capturing the essence of what had occurred to me, for the benefit of all.

Taking up a large sheet of paper I wrote down all that had been presented to my curious mind, and in broad sure strokes, I sketched out a diagram that seemed to capture the essence of what I had seen. Rather than the traditional *horizontal* linear depiction of the autism spectrum, where low-functioning autism sits on one end of the line and high-functioning autism on the other, I saw the whole concept as a *vertical* plumb line with high-functioning autism occurring just below the surface of consciousness, and whose lineal descent into the unconscious was marked out at intervals by *Points of Being* which the individual on the autism continuum inhabited, from high to moderate, and to its most low-functioning expression. In creating this diagram, I began to map out an uncharted way into the deep, unexplored territory of the autistic psyche, in order to reveal its hidden inner-life.

Having sketched my initial insights, I quickly ran through my mind the broad concepts of autism as they are currently understood: cognitive, emotional, social and physical and found myself reinterpreting them all in the light of the intuitive knowledge that I had just received.

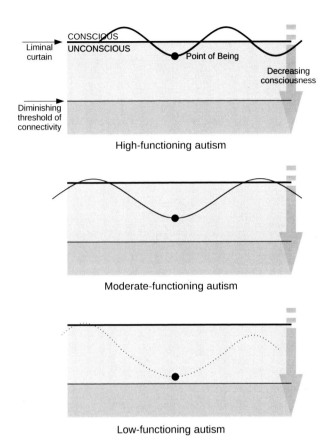

Figure 1 – An alternative form of consciousness and its oscillations

In terms of the oscillation of psychic energy which connects the unconscious and conscious mind, the higher the individual is seated within the unconscious, the higher the frequency, the stronger the connection between the individual's inner and outer world and the higher their functioning; conversely, the lower the individual is seated within the unconscious, the lower the frequency, the weaker the connection between the individual's inner and outer world and the lower their functioning.

By this scale, the overall functioning of an individual on

the autism spectrum is determined by the degree to which they are seated within the unconscious, and by this reckoning, there is a corresponding diminishing threshold of connectivity where the oscillation becomes weak and irregular, rising into consciousness sporadically, until no longer able to rise from the unconscious, weakened as it is, to the point of disintegration. So it is that Pythian Being is seated at descending points on a continuum within the unconscious; their being is pitched at the interface between their personal unconscious and that of the collective unconscious of which they are, to varying degrees, aware.

For the Pythia, their Point of Being, whether high, moderate or low, determines their basic level of conscious awareness. However, within the strata of the unconscious which the individual inhabits there is scope for an increase in conscious awareness, the prerequisite for social awareness, not by being pulled out of their inner world, but rather by being *impelled from within* to rise into consciousness through the therapeutic power of time.

It may be argued that surely this movement of energy between the unconscious and the conscious mind suggests a falling in and out of consciousness in rapid succession, much in the way one might control and release the strings of a marionette, watching it drop in a heap one moment then suddenly spring to life the next. Of course this is an absurd image, so an explanation is needed to clarify nonetheless.

If Pythiism is seated in the unconscious mind, it stands to reason that the psychotypical expression of consciousness, that is, the experience of the greater majority of people, is seated in the conscious mind. This presumption is affirmed by the majority of the population's unfettered interpretation of the world of body language and spoken communication and the general ease of their socialisation.

This distinction is also helpful in describing the point at which psychotypical and Pythian experience converge. The Pythia are constantly springing from the unconscious in their waking hours; psychotypical people also going about their daily business have flashes of access to instincts and material emanating from the unconscious. This is particularly true in the case of synchronicity (where a conscious experience triggers the memory of the contents of a dream). However, the exception proves the rule: unlike the Pythia, whose psychological perception constantly oscillates between two states of consciousness, psychotypical people rarely have free access to the deeper levels of the unconscious, except within their dreams.

First and foremost, Pythiism is a work of depth psychology which turns our attention towards a radically new theoretical framework of interpretation for the condition known as autism, a theory whose premise is based not in the machinations of the brain, but in the operations of the psyche: the combined processes of the unconscious and conscious mind whose individual and collective elements strive towards a state of equilibrium.

Many scientific phenomena, such as the existence of dark matter (that which is unseen but nevertheless makes up the majority of the material universe), can only be inferred through the observation of secondary effects, and so it is in the case of the autism spectrum. The interplay between the unconscious and conscious mind which gives the presentation of autism its particular psychological flavour is observed through the secondary effects of physical presentation and behaviour: the realm of the unconscious being the *dark matter* in which the Pythia live and move and have their Being.

This work entitled Pythiism acknowledges the meticulous observation conducted by researchers who have made the study of autism their life's work, and who have built up the physical and behavioural portrait of the autism spectrum as it is currently understood. The symptoms and behaviour associated with autism still stand, and therefore I do not intend to furnish this work with multiple examples from case studies; for it is from you the reader's own lived and clinical experience that you will be able to test the hypothesis I present. There is no need for me to reinvent the wheel, only to redefine the nature of the load it carries. What I seek to do is to hold in relief that which cannot be pinned down, but can most certainly be observed: the underpinning reality of the unconscious, which informs and shapes autism and its expression of being.

The chapters of this book are organised under the major characteristics of autism, interpreted through the lens of Pythiism: language, cognition, relationships, special interests, sensory sensitivity and movement and coordination. Also included are rarely or never covered areas of autism research: a psycho-evolutionary perspective, the existential emotions, and psychic phenomena and spirituality.

Throughout this book the terms autism/autistic and Pythia/Pythian are used when referring to the collective group and individual person on the autism spectrum, and are often interchangeable, acknowledging the evolutionary nature of language transitioning at the coalface of new discovery. The distinctions made between the various subjects in each chapter are necessary for exploration, but are in many ways artificial, for all its parts constitute an integrated whole, the overlap of categories weaving throughout this work.

My hope is to open a conversation which reframes the current understanding of autism by exploring it broadly within the parameters of Pythiism; to show that this template is in no way inferior to what has come before; that this alternative theory can hold its own when subjected to robust enquiry, and that its implications bear good fruit for therapeutic considerations and outcomes. Indeed, this revolutionary theory holds enormous implications for the treatment of those on the autism spectrum, engendering a seismic shift in focus from empirical to intuitive observation, which will be examined throughout this work.

Pythiism: Reframing autism as an alternative form of consciousness, rose out of the recesses of my heart and mind as the next evolution in our understanding of autism, this work constituting the fourth phase in a decade-long enquiry beginning with my autobiography: *My Autistic Awakening: Unlocking the potential for a life well lived*, my therapeutic work *Contemplative Therapy for Clients on the Autism Spectrum: A Reflective Integration Therapy manual for psychotherapists and counsellors*, and *RIT for kids: Contemplative therapy for Young children on the autism spectrum (ages 5-12)*; now all under the umbrella of works that are Pythiism broadly explored.

Beginning with clinical observation, followed by therapy and now theory, Pythiism finally reveals the complete picture of our understanding of autism, confirming that those on the autism spectrum are not so much *diagnosed* as *discovered*.

Pythiism posits not only an equally valid point of reference for understanding autism to that of a developmental disorder, but also professes a *better one*, uncovering the wisdom of autism – this most misunderstood of conditions – by reinterpreting our understanding of autism in terms of health rather than pathology, by expanding our knowledge exponentially, and advancing new therapeutic modalities which cater to those on the autism spectrum and their alternative form of consciousness – informed by the paradigm shift that is Pythiism.

CHAPTER 1

Autism and its archetype

(autism's incarnation)

It is no easy matter to speak of the unconscious in the language of the everyday, even less so in words couched in the concepts of scientific endeavour. What is needed is to leave mere words behind and reach far back into the primordial first-languages of archetypes, whose symbols and stories continue to furnish humanity with personal and communal truths. Archetypes are awash with all the rich and terrible experiences of humanity: love and sacrifice, death and betrayal, honour and duty, hope and beauty, and above all these, the quest to find meaning in it all.

The unconscious is conservative by nature; that is to say, it has established and steadily preserved over aeons the symbology by which it communicates. Its ancient language is founded on binaries of male and female, darkness and light, good and evil, order and chaos, and it is out of the stability of such concepts that archetypes form.

Carl Jung expressed his concept of archetypes from repeated observations of characters and images manifesting in the myths and fairy tales of world literature. Springing up in all times and places: old women and young maidens, heroes and villains, kings and paupers, humans and beasts, and multitudinous other inherited motifs emanating from the depths of the collective unconscious as recurring patterns within the human psyche.

When considering my new theory of autism, I quickly realised that it was necessary for me to find an archetype, a metaphor that would perfectly frame not only the *symptoms* but also the very *essence* of what I had discovered. This was of great importance to me. For many years, I had been unsatisfied with the way autism had been explained. The question: "What is autism?" had routinely, almost exclusively, been answered in terms of its symptoms (a lack of social understanding, limited ability to partake in reciprocal conversation and limited interests) rather than that of its origin – what it is *in itself*.

In describing a new theory of autism, an archetype rose to give what is unconscious a voice. The image of the Oracle of Delphi – originally titled Pythia – began to take shape in my mind: a solitary female figure, inhabiting neither the world of men nor that of the gods, poised between two realms yet serving both. An archetype, although profoundly symbolic, nevertheless enfleshed in the ancient Greek world in the lives of real women who were chosen and set apart to fulfil a necessary role in society – sacred and prophetic.

Figure 2 – The Pythia of Delphi

Pondering this archetype, the term "Pythiism" sprang to my mind – a neologism that seemed to me worthy of the dignity of those on the spectrum, whose privileged place and prophetic role in society comes as a sudden epiphany. Many psychological conditions have their classical archetypes: Narcissus, Oedipus, Cassandra, Achilles; and now is the time for autism to find *its archetype*, to share its story. In the Pythia, I had found the story of autism and set myself to tell it.

Below is a simple and unvarnished account of the role the Pythia played in the ancient world, for most of the details surrounding the oracular process were held within common knowledge, and have therefore been lost to the mists of time. Nevertheless, her story provides an archetype and template for autism that carves out vast metaphors to encapsulate and carry the intuitive concepts that will be explored throughout this work. Her story will serve to frame the theory of Pythiism, informing the narrative throughout.

Pythia (8th century BC – 4th century AD), was the title conferred upon any woman chosen to serve as high priestess throughout the history of the Temple of Apollo, in Delphi, ancient Greece. On the death of her predecessor, a new priestess of good character and native to Delphi would be selected. This was regardless of marriage, family attachments and individual standing – all were surrendered on becoming the Pythia. The Pythia were chosen from all stratas of society: wealthy or impoverished, young or old, educated or illiterate. Their selection lay not in any particular status, but in the aptitude of the individual woman to fulfil the prophetic role of speaking on behalf of the deity.

The Pythia began as a modestly clothed young virgin, emphasising her purity, setting her apart for union with the divine Apollo. One day, a supplicant visited the temple and beholding her beauty carried her off and violated her. Such was the indignation of the citizens of Delphi that they passed a law forbidding the selection of young virgins, substituting in their stead elderly women fifty years of age to pronounce

the oracles, dressing each in the robes of a young maiden –
recalling the Pythia of old.

The Pythia was famed for her prophecies inspired by the
god Apollo. The authority and prestige of the Pythia was
without peer; she – the most powerful woman of the classic
world. Amongst those who sought her inspired wisdom were
Aristotle, Ovid, Plato and Sophocles. Veiled in purple, she
would perform rites of purification in preparation for her
priestly role. She would undergo a period of fasting, then
bathe in the nearby sacred spring and drink of its holy waters.
Processing along the sacred way with her many companions
holding laurel branches and incanting sacred poems, she
arrived at length at the entrance to the temple, where a
sacrificial goat would be offered.

Removing her veil and clothed in a white garment,
the Pythia would descend alone into the Adyton (Greek
adyton – inaccessible), the deepest and most inaccessible room
within the temple. There she mounted a tripod and sat within
a gilded cauldron, and holding laurel leaves in one hand, and a
shallow dish of spring water into which she gazed in the other,
she pronounced oracles and prophecies of the future. Seated
in her inner sanctum, she would fall into a trance overcome
by the sacred vapours (Greek *pneuma* – breath) emanating
from the chasm below, and speak on behalf of the deity. Her
utterings, sometimes clear, sometimes unintelligible, were
interpreted by the temple priests as the ancient prophecies
of old.

On inhaling the vapours the Pythia's figure seemed to
enlarge, her hair stood on end, her aspect changed and her
voice amplified, seemingly more than human. The supplicant
was allowed to seek the answer to only one question regarding
his fate, after which he was to withdraw immediately from
the temple to live out his destiny as pronounced by the
Pythia. Such were the sheer number of supplicants, that
it was often necessary to engage numerous priestesses to
minister to the many who had made the long and arduous

pilgrimage to the Temple of Apollo.

The Pythia could only be consulted one day a month. Such was her effort that the sessions left her shaking and spent with exhaustion like a marathon runner, or a dancer after a frenzied dance, her life being considerably shortened by the sheer exhaustion exacted by her role. One time, the Pythia was consulted despite the omens being ill-favoured. The temple priests pressed the Pythia to prophesise, resulting in her hysterical collapse and death some days later.

Regarding archetypes, Jung considered them mere forms with no substance of their own, incapable of being made conscious and reflecting nothing bar the collective experience from which they first sprung.

In naming the Pythia as the archetype of those on the autism spectrum, we shall witness a phenomena that Jung himself would have hardly thought possible: the birth of an archetype in real time, a pattern manifesting across the psyche of the whole Pythian population, the Pythia *made conscious*, in the mind of every man, woman and child who bears her nature.

CHAPTER 2

A psycho-evolutionary perspective

(autism as origin)

Recognising autism as an alternative form of consciousness recalibrates our perception regarding its origins. Autism is not a corruption of normal human development, but rather, is the primary expression of human consciousness that first awakened to its potential and purpose.

Following the pattern of all evolutionary processes, human consciousness developed over millennia, beginning as an oscillation of psychic energy between an unconscious and conscious state of awareness, rising from and returning to its creaturely state in increments so subtle, so as to be hardly perceived. Its wavering oscillations, strengthening by degrees, reached at length a *tipping point* in which, sudden awakening was pushed: a psycho-evolutionary event creating for the majority of humanity, consciousness as default.

So it was that humanity first rose from a purely unconscious state, through the influence of millennia of psycho-evolutionary forces, to take their privileged place in attaining consciousness. Human consciousness developed out of the unconscious whose fathomless depths fall away into a vast, ever receding inner-scape containing within it the imprint of all the processes, stages and forms of everything that has come into being.

In order for us to better understand the psycho-evolutionary phenomena that Pythiism expresses, it is crucial that we embrace a fundamental evolutionary truth: that the brain is a *secondary response* to the needs of the psyche, an organism whose development has always been contingent on its demands.

How do we know this to be true? For some billions of years, the simple organisms that pulled themselves through and out of the primordial soup to move about the earth's surface used *sense, feedback and reaction (nerves)*, creating little by little, according to their needs, *a scaffolding (brain)* through which to support *their intentions (psyche)*. The brain therefore, is a physical manifestation of the *intentions of the psyche*: the combined psycho-evolutionary processes of the unconscious and conscious mind, over aeons, bending matter to its will.

The assertion that humanity, over millennia, rose by degrees from a purely unconscious state and assumed consciousness, presents a question for our consideration: Why have the Pythia, although small in number, maintained free access to the unconscious, while the vast majority of humanity have evolved to live, by and large, in the conscious alone? Pythiism has persisted for the same reason all evolutionary factors persist: because it furnishes humanity with qualities that are both needed and desirable.

In the time of the Greek oracles, the Pythia were chosen from all stratas of Delphi's society: wealthy or impoverished, young or old, educated or illiterate. So it is that Pythian individuals spring up spontaneously, born into all ethnic, social, geographical and time settings. Though few in number, rather than being lost in anonymity, the Pythia seem to thrive on the ratio of one-to-many, asserting their influence on a grand scale disproportionate to their numbers through a dominance of thought and creativity emanating from the depths of the unconscious itself.

The Pythia's alternative form of consciousness has persisted and coexisted with the psychotypical expression of human consciousness to fulfil a necessary function in society: to continue to freely access the rich, creative and ample material hidden within the depths of the unconscious, for the good of all.

The Pythian individual, spanning both the unconscious and conscious realms of being, is the custodian of the primary pattern of personhood, whose inner-authority asserts itself in every age and to this day. The energy of autism is dominant, and the energy of autism is dominant because the unconscious is dominant.

Conduits of the unconscious, the Pythia have inherited a unique capacity to harness its forces and channel its creative energies. Their capacity "to turn away from the everyday world", as Hans Asperger put it, has, throughout the whole of human history, never ceased contributing to humanity's whole field of perception: cognitive, emotional, social, physical and spiritual.

So it is that those dwelling within the upper-reaches of the unconscious maintain a lively and enduring connection between the unconscious and conscious aspects of the mind, and in doing so society continues to be greatly enriched. So crucial is the capacity for humanity to maintain its connection to the unconscious in this way, that it more than justifies the presentation, no matter how compromised, of those who dwell in the unconscious' deepest recesses.

As we have previously explored, Pythian Being is seated within descending points on a continuum within the unconscious, exercising a unique expression of human perception, the nature of which dictates the fate of the few and ensures the robustness of the many. It is an *essential* evolutionary trade-off whose psycho-evolutionary advantage pays a high price, manifested in autism's most low-functioning expression.

Seen in this light, the new wave of eugenics that seeks to eliminate autism from the gene pool, rather than being a breakthrough in scientific achievement, becomes at once a dangerous precedent based on a bias. Instead of accepting and allowing, they are rejecting and denying, and it is this lack of trust in the overall pattern of evolutionary events that have brought humanity thus far, that threatens our human existence by seeking to produce future outcomes of which we have no knowledge or control.

Regardless of how deeply they are seated within the unconscious, the dignity of the autistic individual stands, for personhood is rooted not in *doing* but in *being*. Just as there are physical forests whose diverse and myriad ecosystems have formed over many millennia, so too have *the forests of the mind* developed in which everyone has a niche, whose delicate balance is held together by forces that, although beyond our observation, function for our overall good. Put another way, the life of the human race is a richly woven ancient tapestry, each single strand guaranteeing the integrity of the whole. Autism's psycho-evolutionary persistence continues, as it has from the beginning, to shuttle its way between the unconscious and conscious realms of being, strengthening and beautifying the whole fabric of humanity.

CHAPTER 3

The Pythia speaks

(language)

Nowhere is the effect of Pythiism more evident than in its expression of language, filtered as it is through the processes of the unconscious itself. Hans Asperger's astute observation in 1944 that, "They all have one thing in common: the language feels unnatural", perfectly describes those for whom primordial silence is their mother tongue.

In Figure 3 we explore the regression of speech as it moves further away from the Liminal Curtain, the demarcation between unconscious and conscious awareness (which is covered fully in the next chapter).

We have previously examined how the overall functioning of any given individual on the autism spectrum is determined by the point at which they are seated within the unconscious. Each individual expresses not only a greater or lesser connection to conscious awareness, but also a greater or lesser capacity for spoken language. Their position within the unconscious, whether high, moderate or low, likewise determines the quality of their speech. The higher the functioning, the more fluid and accessible the speech; the lower the functioning, the more simple and stilted speech becomes, until the capacity for single words that convey basic needs in single word survival speech are reduced to repetitious non-functional language, sounds and unintelligible words, finally finishing in silence as a result of a diminishing threshold of connectivity to the conscious realm.

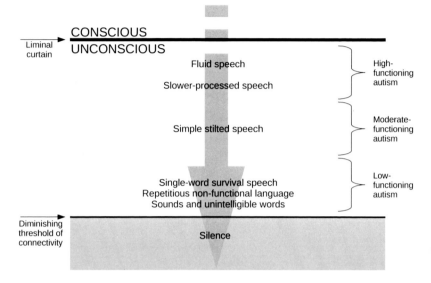

Figure 3 – Descent into the unconscious in speech

The quality of spoken language within the autistic population in both children and many adults often has a "Delphic" quality: portentous in its subject matter, strange in its pitch and earnest in its intent. It is often divorced from social context and uttered in declarations that do not admit the give and take of conversation. Having spoken, the Pythian withdraws once more into their inner world, back to the silence where words cannot come.

Within the context of Pythiism, the quality of speech of those on the autism spectrum makes perfect sense. The conscious mind is the land of spoken language and logic, the unconscious mind the land of symbolic language and intuition. It is the burden of the Pythia to navigate their way between two states of being, constantly crossing the checkpoint between the unconscious and the conscious, the passport of their personhood always at the ready. For them, it is the integration of these two selves that is most at stake.

This is certainly borne out in the high prevalence of delayed speech in autistic children in infancy. This integration often occurs as late as their second or even third year or more, many making their debut by leaving their silent world only to launch into complete and complex sentences whose sudden facility can only be accounted by what I call prior *unconscious cognition*, operating below the level of conscious thought.

For those on the autism spectrum, the execution of speech takes monumental effort. To find one's words is the equivalent of drawing up by hand a bucket of water from a very deep well. The effect of traversing two states of consciousness is more than evident in their tendency towards mutism. Contrary to popular belief, mutism in those on the autism spectrum is not selective, nor is it solely the outcome of the effects of anxiety, for mutism can exist without any trigger for anxiety at all. Rather, mutism – the inability to find one's words – is a manifestation of the difficulty of negotiating two states of consciousness, in which the slower mental processing speed within this population is a symptom. Much in the way a bucket of water drawn from a deep well can hit a snag on its ascent to the surface, so it is with their spoken language: the depth at which the individual resides within the unconscious determines the ease of facility and the rate at which language can be retrieved and spoken.

This rule also applies to their difficulty in repairing a conversation. For those on the spectrum, conversation is not so much an art, as a caving expedition. If the oscillation that draws communication up from the unconscious is disrupted by, for example, another's well-meaning comment, there is often a need to start the thread of conversation all over again. Pythian conversation is drawn up from the depths, and as such, from there it must once again begin its ascent.

This is why active listening skills, so beneficial in counselling the psychotypical client, need to be used, in the case of the Pythian, sparingly, or not at all. Eye contact, murmurs of encouragement, micro-expressions and nodding in agreement, employed singularly or in combination, can be more than enough to disrupt the ascent of what the client is endeavouring to communicate, because the oscillation that carries the content of their communication from the unconscious is also the one that latches onto external sensory information, whose types and effects will be explored later in this book.

In their day-to-day functional language, there is a constant struggle to achieve a state of equilibrium within the operations between the unconscious and the conscious mind. When all other forms of language fail – body language, prosody, pitch, tone and inflection – *bare words themselves* become the bridge between their inner and outer life.

For the Pythia, it is the longest journey from the world of symbols to the world of speech. Seated within the unconscious, their silent world is a vibrant, bubbling cauldron of creative energy. As they rise to meet the world without, something gets lost in translation. The struggle to achieve a constant state of equilibrium across two modes of consciousness comes at great cost, and the cost of harnessing their unconscious to the conscious mind produces a most ingenious method of adaptation: the exchange of fluidity of thought for rigidity of thought. The unconscious, so fluid and intuitive in itself, employs precision and logic as a coping mechanism to anchor itself in a foreign milieu: that of the conscious mind.

The Pythias' speech patterns are often painstakingly precise, and their tendency towards pedantry – an insistence on the law of logic and adherence to the correction of errors above all other social and emotional considerations – masks the intuitive spirit that, ironically, underpins all their contact with the world without.

The oscillation between their two states of consciousness produces yet more curiosities in the way they are are bound to communicate, such as their propensity for unmodulated speech. The often flat and nasal tone of speech synonymous with autism, within the context of Pythiism, can well be reinterpreted as the accent of the unconscious itself, which takes no cues from without. Closely allied to this, their flow of speech runs on quickly without pause, much in the way a rock climber throws a grappling hook with rope attached with all their might, to cover as much distance as possible between them and the rock face they climb. Their unusual inflections often stress almost every syllable, mirroring the steady climb into the world of the spoken word, carefully placing one foot in front of the other as it were, revealing the enormous amount of energy it takes for them to express themselves in the conscious realm.

Talking too much or too little and randomly chopping and changing subject matter during the course of a single conversation too, can be interpreted as artefacts of the continuous oscillation from one state of consciousness to the other. It is like a learner driver crudely crunching gears and pushing pedals haphazardly in an attempt to drive a stretch of unfamiliar road: the route, the journey from the silent landscape of the unconscious; the destination, the bustling metropolis of the conscious mind.

These factors, and more, point to the unconscious overcompensating for its connection with the conscious mind. So it is that the Pythia employ precision in language, the way a blind person uses a white stick, tapping away with speech in bursts of interaction invited and uninvited, as they try to navigate the social environs of the conscious world. Odd prosody, pedantry and precision – it is all of a piece. It is the presence of the unconscious doing its best to express itself in a language that is not its own.

Literal interpretation is a prime example of the struggle the unconscious undergoes to engage in the land of conscious language, stubbing its metaphorical toe on sarcasm, idioms, and figures of speech. As a child the expression, "keep your eyes peeled" used to send shivers up my spine! And therein lies the clue to its origin. The unconscious speaks in symbols and pictures and carries this template over to the conscious mind. It cannot suppress its own language and grafts it straight onto figures of speech, galvanising graphic images onto mere words. So fundamental is this artefact of the unconscious that it persists into adulthood, penetrating the firewall of the intellect each and every time an idiom is presented to the conscious mind.

Once we understand autism as an oscillation between the unconscious and conscious mind, the profile of singular peculiarities observed in autistic speech and language resonate as a whole and finally fit together, as we shall also see in the following examples.

It is a curiously common observation that many individuals with autism fail to absorb the local accent of the community in which they are raised. Their vocabulary, although often impressive in its scope and of the highest technical specificity, remains strangely resistant to the patterns and inflections of speech to which they are constantly exposed. Their speech often reflects the linguistic flavour of one who has learned their phraseology, not from hearing it spoken, but straight out of the pages of a book of a lost language, their over-precise diction demonstrating how foreign the cadences of their local spoken language actually are to them. Again, these tendencies are determined by the best efforts of the unconscious to interpret a language that is not its own, before falling back again into its symbolic world, continually wiping the capacity for living accents to stick.

What is stranger is the Pythia's propensity for the accents of the dead! Many are given to archaic language and highfalutin phraseology: ornate, florid and flowery, as if straight out of the pages of a Victorian novel. Many of those on the spectrum have a strong sense of affinity for a bygone era, their numbers well represented in Victorian re-enactment weekends and Renaissance fairs, mistakenly attributed by the casual observer as a form of escapism from the randomness of modern living to the highly structured society of a genteel past – but it is not escapism.

This presumption hides a far more fundamental principle at play: the unconscious prefers old to new, ancient to modern, and the Pythian individual has access to the contents of the collective unconscious, the storehouse of the collective human experiences of the past, whose roots reach far back into the primordial silence of humanity itself, awaking to its potential and purpose. What motivates their enthusiasm for "living history" and is reflected in their cadences of their speech, is their ability to intuit the collective experience of the last five hundred years or so, still in the shallows, still accessible to those for whom the unconscious is their native home.

The volume of their spoken word, too, has its tale to tell. To listeners, it can be perceived as either too loud or too soft. More often than not, their speech is considered far too loud for context, as if attempting to communicate across a large distance, when all the while the recipient of the conversation is standing in close proximity. As comical as this scenario seems, nevertheless it mirrors the fundamental position of the Pythia: their lives are seated in the unconscious, and it is from out of these depths that all their communication flows. The volume of their speech is itself an artefact of the unconscious desiring to be heard over the greatest of all distances – from that of the world *within* to that of the world *without*.

This alternative form of consciousness is also responsible for the peculiarities in their auditory perception and the distortions that ensue. Granted, the presence of many voices in a room can cause confusion in the Pythian individual, whose attention simultaneously locks onto all available detail with each rising oscillation into the conscious mind. Be that as it may, the distortion of auditory perception can persist for them in a conversation between themselves and one other within a quiet environment. For them, one of their most frequent responses to a question out of the blue is "Sorry?" They hear the *sound* of the question, but in a garbled unintelligible form, prompting them to ask for it to be repeated.

It is not that they cannot interpret what is said, but the rising and falling oscillation between the unconscious and conscious mind, can take with it fragments of sounds and words dissolving them, leaving half a message that needs to be picked up on a second or third hearing to fully interpret the conversation at hand. When not engaged in a conversation, Pythians tend to power down, taking their seat more snugly in the unconscious, their abiding home. It is from there that the spoken word comes to them in distorted form, and from there they rise once again into the state of consciousness to attend to what is said.

Closely related to this constant need to attend, is their need to vocalise their thoughts. That this helps them consolidate their comprehension of a concept, question or thought is not in dispute. What I would like to draw attention to is the reason why they feel the need to do so. Quite simply, vocalising their thoughts employs the conscious mind to make it clearer to the unconscious mind what is going on, spanning the distance between their two modes of perception – a truly *internal dialogue*. They are quite capable of *thinking* their thoughts, but it is like having the volume on a radio turned down too low in a room to take in what is being said. Vocalising their thoughts is like turning up the volume so that all in the room can comfortably hear. In this case, the *all* refers to a listening audience of two – the unconscious and conscious mind tuned in together.

During conversation, their need to vocalise their thoughts or questions from others, is often linked to a corresponding need for short periods of silence. What to an observer can look like the need to "gather one's thoughts", belies a different quality of processing altogether. The Pythian is not so much *thinking* of what to say, but rather, *retrieving* what to say. Between the two there is a qualitative difference. In clinical sessions, having asked a question, I have noted the following "oracular" behaviour: the bowing of the head and lowering of the eyes while the client waits for the response to come, and when it comes, it often rises all of a piece and complete – it is a physical manifestation of knowledge drawn straight from the unconscious mind to be disseminated through the processes of conscious thought.

Drawing on the archetype of the Pythia of Delphi sheds more light on how the Pythia expend their psychic energy when we recall that she could only be be consulted one day a month, and that the effort of her sessions left her shaking and spent with exhaustion like a marathon runner, or a dancer after a frenzied dance, her life being considerably shortened by the sheer exhaustion exacted by her role.

Those on the autism spectrum are indeed consumed by the effort needed to traverse their two states of consciousness, with the additional burden of having to navigate particularly the emotional and social aspects of their daily lives. It is little wonder, therefore, that the enormous effort required for the Pythia to communicate should produce all sorts of creative ways to conserve their mental energy.

Among the most familiar of these strategies is their propensity for repetitive speech. When the currency of speech is so costly, why not have a handful of stock-standard words and phrases at the ready? Of course, this is not a conscious habit, as anyone on the end of an autistic monologue would know. Even those seated higher within the unconscious are quite capable of getting stuck in a mental loop, quite literally, as their thought processes spring from the unconscious to the conscious and back again, in a self-renewing cycle.

The Pythian mind is very adept at recycling indeed. There can be a tendency to palilalia – the repetition of one's own words, the individual's repetition of speech mirroring the oscillations between their unconscious and conscious mind. That the words or expressions may be important or in some way pleasing to the speaker by dint of their novelty, can extend the repetition, as if reconfirming the *actuality* of the statement rather than for purposes of clarification.

Another way in which they employ what I term *linguistic*

recycling, is in developing a sudden special interest in a single word or phrase, using it in and out of context at will. Once a Pythian finds an expression that pleases them, they are likely to recycle its usage, repeating it in and out of context, not only for ease and expediency of communication but also for the sheer pleasure of the sound of it ascending once again into the realm of the conscious mind.

There is also their propensity for echolalia – the repetition of another's words rather than one's own. In what way are we to interpret this phenomenon? It is of a different order than that of the joy of constantly repeating to oneself a pleasing word or phrase. Echolalia is a true artefact of the unconscious, a "sound check" for the process of spoken language at the coalface of conscious speech.

Despite its inherent difficulties, those on the spectrum have nothing short of a life-long love affair with language, relishing words, their nuances, usage and origins, their shapes, sounds and textures. Not content to simply enjoy the words that they hear, they are renowned for inventing their own – neologisms, new words and expressions full of the creativity of the unconscious – descriptive, quirky and highly original. My own child, a past master of neologisms, told me once that he had been given a "twirly-whirly lock" (combination lock) for his school locker, and when walking with him, telling him of my difficulty in "keeping up" with him, he said with some exasperation, "I have a hard time keeping down with you!"

A conspicuous tendency, particularly in Pythian children, is to say a word or phrase out loud that invokes fits of laughter, but whose comical significance is directed at and shared with no one but themselves, the effect of which is constantly renewed every time it is uttered: a rolling punch line of a private joke for a captive audience of one! The significance of this behaviour too has its roots deep within the alternative form of consciousness that the Pythia possess. The oscillation carries a quirky concept from the unconscious into conscious awareness, presenting it as springing fresh and new into thought with every cycle, a self-renewing sense of the ridiculous! Moreover, it is not strictly *one* who is the happy recipient of such mirth, but *two*. The private joke is whispered, as it were, by the unconscious to cascade in laughter throughout the conscious mind.

That Pythian humour is idiosyncratic by nature is without question, but it is of a flavour that demands closer investigation. Much of their sense of humour revolves around language and wordplay and can be universally defined as having something of a surreal quality: strange, dreamlike and irrational. These underpinning qualities come as no surprise, for it is out of the creativity of the unconscious itself that they emerge. Among the Pythia there is a leaning towards the bizarre, flirting at the threshold where language and meaning break down. It is no mistake that their humour is dark humour, skirting as it does the dark recesses of the unconscious mind where the threshold of connectivity is weakened to the point of disintegration.

When it comes to their taste in humour, theirs is a brave approach, finding mirth where few would expect it to exist. To find the flavour of joy in words at the point where they seem to disappear into meaninglessness affirms a great hope: that meaning can be retrieved right out of the mouth of chaos itself, in the existence of an order that ultimately has the last laugh.

And so it is with confidence and compassion that I follow the plumb line of Pythiism as far as I am able, tracing the oscillations as they falter and fall away into the very depths of the unconscious to rise no more. Many of the Pythia emerging from their prolonged silence in early childhood to take their place in the world of spoken language and literature, whereas others lose their first faltering words and go back to their silent world never to return.

Pythiism is described as personhood seated in the unconscious, and this description pertains especially to those who are seated in its deepest recesses. Observing the non-functional and unintelligible language of those who manifest Pythiism's most low-functioning expression, one is confronted with a hard truth: you cannot attribute meaning to words where no meaning exists. To do so is to dishonour their lives by refusing to accept the reality of their state. But this reality should not be cause for despair.

How can we justify this hope? In losing or never attaining consciousness, nevertheless, their individual dignity stands, for as we have previously explored, personhood is rooted not in *doing* but in *being*. Those who abide in the deepest recesses of the unconscious live a perennial dream-state and so are spared the anxiety, depression and lack of self-esteem so evident in those who are seated highest in the unconscious, for their ego is simply too fractured to stand outside of themselves to regard their *self* as a separate entity to be anxious, depressed or lacking in self-esteem. But they do have a *self*, although not expressed, which is kept safe in the Mystery who calls order out of chaos. And in the meantime they are not consigned to the shadows, for they walk among us, nor are they without advocate, for those seated in the upper reaches of the unconsciousness are their voice.

We have explored how the fundamental effort required for the Pythia to express spoken language can be attributed to the depth at which they are seated within the unconscious. So precise is this phenomenon, that even before the evidence of behaviour, the degree to which the individual is seated within the unconscious can be almost always ascertained through speech alone.

CHAPTER 4

The liminal curtain

(cognition)

I admit that in approaching the subject of cognition as it pertains to the Pythia, I do so with some hesitation, perhaps in part due to the connotation it holds in terms of measuring or even showcasing their intelligence, or highlighting that which escapes them in terms of their failure to grasp the big picture and the curious gulf between the two. Speaking for myself, I am quite in two minds about the subject, and will therefore begin with those two minds as my starting point for exploring Pythiism's cognitive profile.

The dynamic interplay between Pythiism's two states of consciousness is best described by a concept I call the Liminal Curtain (Latin *limen* – threshold). Their fundamental cognitive experience is one of being in constant flux, passing through the curtain that separates the unconscious and the conscious mind in an elegant and ongoing cycle that determines the nature of their cognitive perception.

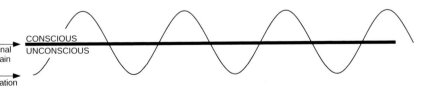

Figure 4 – The liminal curtain

Just as the Pythia of Delphi removed her veil and descended into the deepest room within the temple, so do the Pythia with every oscillation pass through the liminal curtain as they descend again and again to take their solitary seat in the realm of the unconscious. This fundamental flavour of *solitude* for which those on the autism spectrum are known, is often referred to as being *withdrawn*, and withdrawn they are, back into their inner-world where they are not only refreshed, but also empowered to rise once again through the liminal curtain to meet the world without.

The way in which Pythian development differs from that of psychotypical childhood development, is that it incorporates a greatly extended period of inner-calibration between the unconscious and conscious mind, causing a necessary delay in the rate at which milestones of social interaction occur. This process of knitting together the two halves of the Pythian psyche requires the conservation of mental energy, allowing the delicate thread of oscillating psychic energy, at first tenuous and fragile, to strengthen and calibrate throughout childhood, into adolescence and finally consolidate in adulthood.

There are obvious markers of this extended period of development in young Pythian children, such as their silent reserve and preference for solitary activities. Young children on the autism spectrum are said to live *in a world of their own*, and that is exactly where they need to be for their ongoing developmental wellbeing.

The Pythian population's almost universal aversion to eye contact is in direct response to a mind that is not ready or able to fully process and filter the onslaught of material from the conscious world to which they are constantly exposed.

The ongoing developmental processes within the psyche of the Pythian child are as dynamic as they are hidden. As such, parents and professionals can work with this knowledge by welcoming this presentation of autistic interiority as a marker of the child's natural disposition and rate of development.

The continual passing between two states of consciousness produces some very curious cognitive artefacts that are worthy of exploration. The Pythian's conscious mind may be willing enough to take in all the fleeting impressions offered to it, but it is the unconscious mind that meticulously and earnestly sorts, grades and stores away all these hard-won precious pieces of information from above with miserly zeal.

The expression "first impressions count" succinctly sums up the cognitive aspects of how their mind perceives and stores new information when it first connects with the conscious world. The primary oscillation rises to receive the unfamiliar and carries it swiftly away into the depths of the unconscious below, seeking to build as quickly as possible an impression of what has been learned. This primary function of "Unconscious Cognition" can be likened to a librarian working deep within the subterranean caverns of the British Library, whose constant task is to methodically categorise and confirm all the material presented from above.

The Pythia's need to continually piece together what is learned across two states of mind by way of categorisation creates an interesting artefact in the process – their propensity for associational thought. The mind marshals what it knows and runs an inventory through the descending levels of the unconscious in ever decreasing degrees of relevance. This also presents a suitable explanation for why the autistic mind runs so hot, and the individual's constant complaint that they can "never stop thinking" because they are constantly sorting material presented to their mind.

The Pythian tendency to seek precision in all aspects of knowledge, too, is a function of the unconscious' need to maintain a firm grasp on what it understands to be so. A recent and *timely* example of this need came by way of one young client, who on hearing me say that it was a quarter past two, corrected my miscalculation, declaring it to be 2.14pm and thirty seconds. "You're quite right", I said. And so he was.

It is a curious phenomenon to consider the kind of social exchange when a Pythian customer walks into a bar, which goes something like this:

"Can I have a Cola please?"
"Diet?"
"No, I haven't got the willpower."

In this and many other similar scenarios are examples of this alternative form of consciousness. This sudden shift in context may sound comical, but the enormity of the misunderstanding within this exchange manifests the presence of an artefact produced by the descending oscillation passing through the liminal curtain, wiping social context along with it.

Let us now explore certain key aspects of Pythian cognition conceptually known as executive functioning – the orchestration of the broad categories of cognitive processing.

There is a tendency towards impulsivity in Pythian children, particularly in social settings: blurting out whatever comes to mind without giving due consideration to the social consequences of what is said and done. My interest in this tendency however, is not in their inability to suppress their thoughts and observations, but rather, the origin of this raw feed that emanates from such children and adults alike.

There is a saying, "To the innocent, all things are innocent" and this aphorism helps to furnish us with a fundamental understanding of the nature of the unconscious mind: its naivety; that is to say, the unconscious exhibits, by nature, a childlike trustfulness and lack of guile. Let us explore this further by returning once again to the story of the Pythia: in choosing a new priestess in the service of Apollo, great emphasis was placed on her purity. Even the elderly women of fifty dressed in the robes of a young maiden, expressing the innocence of youth. The Pythia, as the collective expression of an archetype, too, exhibit the Delphic qualities of innocence and naivety, regardless of their age and life experience, seated as they are within the unconscious.

We are not at war with the unconscious, neither is the unconscious out to get us or looking to trip us up; rather, what it seeks is to be in fruitful dialogue with the conscious mind, to make itself understood, and in the Pythias' case, to achieve an integrated harmony between their mind's two states. This is not as straight forward a proposal as one would hope, for the conscious mind inhabits the land of logic, the unconscious, the land of symbols. The first is political, the latter, primal.

Pythian social commentary may sound harsh and *impulsive* to our ears, but only in so far that, as a society, we are not in the way of accepting brutal honesty and its prophetic qualities. They are not entering into social exchanges with an eye to *how does this affect me?* Rather, their unvarnished observations speak of a thirst for knowledge through direct enquiry and the raw innocence of those whose only quest is to seek truth. As it was for the philosophers who sought the Pythia's prophecies, so it is for those who enquire of the Pythia today – they get the answer coming to them!

Now let us appraise what is generally described as working memory, that is, the ability to maintain a chain of thought relevant to a specific task at hand, by reframing it within the understanding of Pythiism as an alternative form of consciousness. Given the continual oscillation between what is consciously perceived and what is not, it is no wonder that they have difficulty holding together disparate pieces of information just formed. This cognitive dynamic explains the tendency in Pythian children and some adults to interrupt conversations and their desperate insistence on sharing what they have to say, before their train of thought is disrupted by passing over the threshold into the unconscious below.

The Pythia also experience challenges with problem-solving strategies, whose origins can be pinpointed in the process of the ascending and descending oscillation itself. The enormous distance between the realm of the unconscious in which they are seated and the necessity of operating within the conscious mind coordinates a process of oscillation that, to conserve psychic energy, seeks the path of least resistance. This requirement for their cognitive processing to take the shortest route can result in the kind of rigid thinking that is often noted in autistic children and some adults. It can be frustrating for others to witness their difficulty in changing their hard-won assumptions, doggedly clinging to a strategy long after it has proved fruitless. However, the gradual strengthening of the oscillation that connects their two modes of mind usually ensures an overall improvement in flexible thinking over time.

The oscillation between their unconscious and conscious mind also covers aspects of their trouble with organisational skills and time-management, which fall under the umbrella of knowing how to prioritise. No sooner has the ascending oscillation risen into consciousness and latched onto a task, it descends once again before the Pythian individual is able to consider a course of action.

However, the crux of the matter is not that the Pythian mind does not know how to prioritise, but rather, that it prioritises everything! The ascending oscillation rises into conscious awareness simultaneously locking on to everything in sight, whether relevant or redundant to its needs, and attempts to carry it back into the unconscious, creating a bottleneck that causes the flow of information to freeze up like an overloaded computer. This goes a very long way in explaining the panic and procrastination that sets in the moment they are required to clean their room, or later in life, to sort their paperwork.

Nevertheless, when it comes to creative and inspired thinking, the Pythian mind really comes into its own, having a genius for dispensing altogether with that which would block its free flow of thought, by electing to remain seated within the unconscious in order to ponder a problem or to hatch a creative work.

When met with a perplexing problem to solve, it is the unconscious that takes the reigns. Some of the best problem solving skills happen below the level of consciousness. They entrust to the unconscious that which seems unsolvable to conscious perception. In their waiting we witness a rare quality of patience rivalling even that of the ancient Greek philosophers themselves: prepared to wait as they will, sometimes for decades, for the answer to reveal itself to their conscious mind.

In the classroom setting, over and again we see Pythian students solving extremely curly mathematical problems, and when the delighted teacher asks how they came to their conclusion, they are met with the response, "I don't know." That is to say, *That part of me that is conscious did not arrive at the answer.*

The autistic child's capacity to take in minute detail is, of course, undisputed, but time and again what is also clear is that both children and many adults on the spectrum struggle to make sense of the big picture, termed weak central coherence. They fail to grasp the overall context of their surroundings and struggle to understand its social and learning markers in a cohesive way as would a psychotypical child viewing the whole within a seamless context.

For the Pythia, the oscillation of energy passing through the liminal curtain into consciousness receives its hyper-focused and fleeting impressions of the conscious world before falling back into the unconscious below: the extreme degree of focus is an artefact of the brevity of the oscillation within the conscious realm, explaining the phenomenon known as weak central coherence.

Conversely, we see in the Pythia an incredible capacity for long-term memory. Impressions laid down, even those obtained in infancy, can be retrieved in all their pristine detail at will and for decades to come. There seem too, to be certain details in which the unconscious takes a marked interest, conferring on them an unusual value, storing them away with particular care.

Their acuity for detailed memory, especially that laid down in early childhood, is made possible by a number of factors. Their early perception of consciousness begins as the ascending (albeit weak) oscillation pushes through the liminal curtain revealing, in fragmented fashion, the world of matter in all its novelty. The hit and miss nature of conscious perception in their early childhood guarantees that the first impressions garnered by the conscious mind will be of an unusually strong and lasting quality. This explains why a single, seemingly obscure incident in the life of a Pythian infant can be retained in all its freshness, to be suddenly recalled years later to the amazement of parents – for them, first impressions count!

This mode of perception also accounts for the way in which Pythian children in infancy view objects in parts rather than wholes. The ascending oscillation metes out the psychic energy available to it to take in what is possible, building by degrees and over time, a three dimensional image of the object of their fascination. Rather than being an affliction, this necessary curtailing of view is a source of the most sublime pleasure, and a joy and freshness recaptured in adulthood in pastimes such as model trains and jewellery making, painting toy soldiers and admiring action figures, whose minutiae bring back the bliss of that first fleeting glimpse of the world without.

The capacity for visual memory so remarkable among those on the spectrum has its origin, as well, in the world of the unconscious whose primary language is pictorial. Their ability to think in pictures of the most extraordinary detail is facilitated and strengthened by the visual language employed by the unconscious; in others words, the capacity for visual acuity is shared both by the unconscious and conscious mind.

Given their high degree of focus and precision facilitated by the ascending oscillation, many Pythian individuals express their creativity by rendering the most exquisite detail in fine art, craftsmanship, engineering, music, mathematics and disciplines of all kinds. Moreover, many of humanities' greatest scientific breakthroughs have hung almost exclusively on that peculiar predilection for focusing on minute detail to the exclusion of surroundings, safety, friendships and even personal hygiene: they came, they saw, they conquered!

The Pythian mind is marked by an insatiable curiosity, for they come into this world taking nothing of their experience for granted, and never do. However, to focus unduly on the intelligence of those on the spectrum above other facets of their make-up, to my mind, rather misses the point. Aristotle, Ovid, Plato and Sophocles did not make the long and arduous pilgrimage to Delphi to witness the Pythia's intelligence, for they had plenty of their own! No, they came to seek her wisdom. The Pythia's alternative form of consciousness, their being *seated within the unconscious*, allows them to access – first hand – the wisdom of the ages, effervescing from deep within the collective experience of humanity, for the enrichment of all.

Viewed within the framework of an alternative form of consciousness, those on the autism spectrum can no longer be regarded from a cognitive point of view as limping along in a psychotypical world, but rather, can be respected like seasoned maritime explorers piloting the deepest oceans and avoiding being dashed upon the rocks in the shallows: such is their capacity to navigate with skill and endurance the vast distance between their two states of self.

CHAPTER 5

The existential emotions

(anxiety, anger, guilt)

Since autism's traits have been studied, much has been written regarding the autistic individual's experience of emotions as defined in terms of what they seem incapable of feeling: an incapacity to make contact with a sliding scale of subtle emotions, or what little emotion they can muster seen in terms of low-resolution outputs such as feeling happy, sad, angry or scared.

However, within this elusive affective terrain, two emotional states have been consistently noted and acted upon in terms of therapeutic focus: those of anxiety and anger. Many programmes have been specifically designed to explore anxiety and anger – emotions that seem to define much of the autistic response to both social and environmental input, emotional states often and understandably couched in the context of justifiable reactions to experiences of bullying, social and sensory issues, and other challenges that present themselves on a daily basis.

Given how logical the explanation of such emotions may seem, the very logic applied to these states only serves to cloud our understanding of their origin, shutting down further enquiry by consigning them to categories of *mood disorder*, and neatly reducing them to common clinical considerations of *anxiety disorder* and *anger management.*

However reasonable the consensus formed around the troubles inherent in their day-to-day interactions, it is strange, nonetheless, to note that for those on the autism spectrum, these primary emotions of anxiety and anger so intensely expressed curiously persist, regardless of the high degree of stimulus that would normally be needed to maintain them. This observation is of critical importance in understanding the emotional landscape that those on the autism spectrum inhabit. Moreover, from my extensive experience within the clinical setting, I would add a third to these primary emotions – that of guilt.

Acknowledging and notwithstanding the experience that every person has in terms of their own personal anxiety, anger and guilt and plethora of all manner of emotions produced as a direct consequence of their actions, inactions and being acted upon, those on the autism spectrum often find themselves fishing for reasons as to why they feel perennially angry, anxious or guilty. Casting around for answers to their agitated moods, they seek to attribute them to a perceived injustice, such as being judged by a peer, or saying the wrong thing, and yet find no causal link. Such efforts are an exercise in futility, because we are not dealing with the world of logic, so the tools of logic cannot hope to put emotions to rest.

The question that arises in relation to these three-fold emotions is, from where comes the fuel capable of maintaining such fires? I am convinced that the emotions of anxiety, anger and guilt synonymous with the autistic experience do not have their origin in the brain, but rather, in the psyche, emanating as existential emotions from the depths of the collective unconscious itself. The affective dispositions of anxiety, anger and guilt emanate from within the unconscious: raw, intense and primal, and it is only from their place within the unconscious that they can hope to be integrated.

The conscious mind is the land of everyday living, and the unconscious the refuge of times past. In the conscious mind the Pythia's emotions are their own; in the unconscious, the existential emotions of anxiety, anger and guilt rise up of their own accord out of the collective experience. Some Pythia are more attuned to anxiety, others anger and others still, guilt. What is imperative to their emotional wellbeing, is that the nature of these collective emotions be properly understood.

The emotional dispositions of anxiety, anger and guilt, manifest as an archetypal pattern – repeating without exception – across the whole Pythian population. Each of the three dispositions mark a psycho-evolutionary turning point within human consciousness, tracing our human awakening all the way back to its primordial beginnings. The Pythia are a living testimony to our evolutionary past and a prophetic voice for its future.

Each existential emotion marks a seismic shift in humanity's evolving consciousness, each state rising from earliest to latest in an unbroken chain of becoming. The struggle towards personal and collective maturity is characterised by the trajectory of the three fundamental existential emotions: anxiety, anger and guilt, and their three corresponding transformations into freedom, responsibility and trust, which we shall now briefly explore.

Anxiety (freedom)

Anxiety is often described as an animal emotion, one marked by a basic instinct for survival. Certainly, anxiety in all its hyper-vigilance is the hallmark of the primitive fears of our ancestors. However this state of fear and overwhelming apprehension far predates that of our early ancestors being chased down by the ubiquitous tiger in the jungle. Human anxiety, in its most fundamental expression, marks the evolutionary fate of being pulled out of the mire of a purely creaturely existence into consciousness, with all the uncertainty and myriad of choices that came with so great a freedom.

Our rise from the unconscious into conscious awareness did not leave the apprehensions of creaturely life behind, but folded them into the human psyche, to be forever carried as a reminder of this great achievement. A reminder of our capacity to transcend the limitations of our creaturely existence, inspiring us by the evolutionary striving of aeons that brought us to such a point, that we may not grow tired of carrying the burden laid upon our shoulders that we call *human development*.

Anger (responsibility)

The outrage and indignation synonymous with the raw energy of anger, too, has its origins in the cataclysmic event of human consciousness. The sudden awakening of humankind sent psycho-evolutionary shock-waves reverberating throughout the fabric of human nature, a "rude awakening" of cosmic proportions expressed in the newly awakened as anger. Robbed of mere creatureliness, humanity could never return again to its former state, untroubled by nothing bar the avoidance of death, and it is this cataclysmic event that continues to fuel human anger.

Built into the emergence of the human condition is the responsibility for each and every individual to forever become more than what they first were: an open-ended invitation to transcend their limitations, to carry the heavy burden of conscious life and to carry it well.

Guilt (trust)

More subtle in its manifestation than the preceding disposi-tions, guilt moves as a kind of quiet and searching shadow, suggesting a disharmony between what humanity is and what humanity is capable of becoming. From a psycho-evolutionary perspective, guilt is the fine dust that settles in the aftermath of human awakening, settling over conscious awareness and showing in relief the limitations not only inherent within the human condition as a whole, but also painfully and personally felt at the individual level. Manifesting as a sense of isolation, this existential burden is lightened by the repair mechanism that is "service to others" through which we begin to trust this life that we live.

Exploring these three-fold affective emotional patterns from the perspective of an evolving consciousness redefines the existential emotions of anxiety, anger and guilt within the Pythian population not as mood disorders, but as dispositions in line with their perceptual awareness, allowing them to make *good contact* with the emotions to which they are, by dint of their being seated within the unconscious, predisposed.

The liminal curtain, the demarcation between the unconscious and conscious mind, not only facilitates and regulates their movement between one aspect of consciousness and the other, but also provides a radically counter-intuitive function: that of psychological protection. The way in which the Pythia perceive the existential emotions as an archetypal pattern points to the protective function of the liminal curtain curating the experience of countless generations within the collective unconscious, bundling their experience into solid *types* so as to limit the individual Pythia's degree of exposure to the emotions of the legion within. The Pythia's enhanced access to the existential emotions of anxiety, anger and guilt accounts for what is often mistakenly perceived by others as the limited emotional bandwidth available to them.

Subtle, shifting and of the moment, the emotional states of psychotypical individuals mainly originate in the conscious mind, and although the Pythia have their own degree of access, it is the psychotypical population who have evolved to take their emotional cues in the conscious world and are therefore most predisposed to its malleable emotional terrain. Nevertheless, the existential emotions of anxiety, anger and guilt are the imprint and struggle of every human being that has ever lived and will ever live.

The Pythia of Delphi witnessed the streaming multitudes from the four corners of the ancient world arriving at the Temple of Apollo, bringing their burdened minds and burning questions: so it is that those on the autism spectrum continue to bear witness to the ongoing psycho-evolutionary event of humanity's struggle to accept the burden of human Being.

The Pythia, with all their perceived limitations, stand not at the fringes, but at the epicentre of human experience. Their alternative form of consciousness not only allows them to fully embrace their creaturely anxieties, but also offers them a rare quality of compassion, enabling them to carry the weight of their own existence with courage and endurance over the whole arc of their lifespan: a transforming crucible whose alchemy converts anxiety into freedom, anger into responsibility and guilt into trust – first for themselves and then for all.

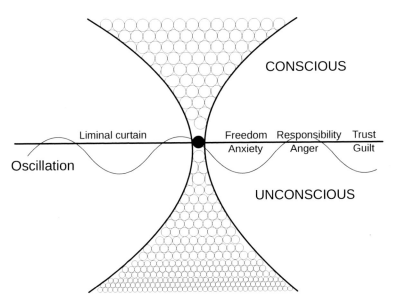

Figure 5 – The alchemy of transforming the existential emotions

CHAPTER 6

Consulting the Pythia

(relationships)

In no area of their presentation are those on the autism spectrum more mysterious and more misunderstood than that of the nature of their relationships. In earliest childhood it appears as though they relate to *nothing*, when in fact they relate to *everything*.

There is an order and progression within their relationships, a slowly unfolding sequence that mirrors the oscillation rising from and returning to the unconscious mind. This pan-relational waveform ascends in infancy, continues to rise in youth, plateaus in mid-life and begins its slow descent with age, returning to the unconscious from which it first sprung.

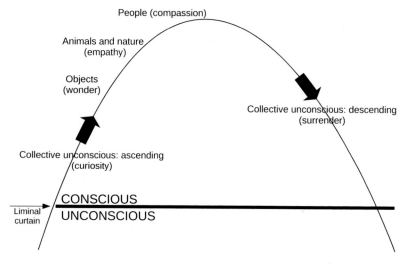

Figure 6 – Trajectory of the relational arc

The trajectory of this relational arc across the Pythian lifespan is divided into five distinct levels and their corresponding dispositions:

- Relationship to the collective unconscious: ascending (curiosity)

- Relationship to objects (wonder)

- Relationship to animals and nature (empathy)

- Relationship to people (compassion)

- Relationship to the collective unconscious: descending (surrender)

The first four levels of their relationships are negotiated from early childhood to the end of adolescence. Some on the spectrum pass through these levels earlier, some later, and some not at all, depending on how deeply they are seated within the unconscious, allowing for the developmental variations from one individual to another.

A glance at these five levels reveals in startling relief their relationship to people coming in at fourth position. This undoubtedly raises the question, "Is a Pythias' capacity to relate to a fellow human being trumped by their ability to connect with a cat, a tree or a train?" Such an interpretation, although somewhat ludicrous, contains within it a fundamental insight into Pythian relationships: they cannot be rushed, rather they are quietly and patiently forged by way of a psycho-relational progression, from one level to the next, whose greatest work and highest point culminates in their relationship to people.

The framework in which we will explore Pythian relationships across the lifespan will include the nature of each level of psycho-relational development, the importance of allowing each stage to progress unhindered from one level to the next, and each level being incorporated along the way, which brings about the integration of each within the whole relational arc.

Relationship to the collective unconscious: ascending (curiosity)

The first level of Pythian psycho-relational development is defined by the individual's relationship to the collective unconscious from which they ascend. Being seated *just below* the surface of consciousness could give the impression of having barely dipped one's toe into the unfathomable waters of the unconscious. However, to be seated on the *other side* of consciousness, even at its threshold, is to dwell far beneath.

The unconscious, as we have explored, connects individual and generational lives whose roots reach far back into the primordial beginnings of life itself, awakening to its potential and purpose. Those on the autism spectrum are custodians of the psycho-evolutionary processes of aeons and as such, their ascending journey from the realms of the unconscious in infancy has a sacred quality, slowly unfolding at their own pace and in their own time.

As the individual begins to rise from the deep recesses of the unconscious, they are met with the vibrant and psychedelic qualities produced by the contents of the unconscious as they near its upper reaches, the place where dreams and the surreal are fashioned. Here, fragmented images, rich and florid, as well as fleeting emotions effervescing from the deeper layers of the unconscious, continue to enthral, fascinate and captivate their curiosity and attention.

The Pythian child begins to be drawn into the realm of consciousness by the curiosity that comes from their first fleeting glimpses gained as they pass through the liminal curtain, receiving both novel and distorted impressions of the sensory world of sight, sound, smell, touch and taste. Their natural curiosity pivots between one realm and the next, the one beneath and the one above the liminal curtain, giving the casual observer the impression of them being *there* one moment and *gone* the next.

Pythian progress at this *ascending* stage of their psycho-relational development, to my observation, is the most robust of all the levels; the one in which the individual is least prone to stall; for the Pythia are not *pulled out* of their inner world, rather they are *impelled from within* to rise into consciousness. The unconscious is dominant, and as such, the pace at which the individual first ascends into consciousness is set by the unconscious itself, which to my mind comes as a great consolation: you can't prevent them from falling, but you can't stop them from rising!

Relationship to objects (wonder)

The second level of Pythian psycho-relational development is distinguished not by their relationship to their mother, but to the world of matter, and it is this necessary stage in Pythian development that constitutes the greatest scandal in those for whom interpersonal relationships are all in all, for it is precisely at this point that those on the spectrum manifest the most subtle of all their relationships, evidenced in the young autistic child's relationship to inanimate objects. Unfortunately, this demonstration of Pythian progress is universally regarded as a horrifying regression, and is often the trigger for *early intervention* programmes, whose overarching focus is aimed at accelerating social interaction.

So curious and so misunderstood is this phenomenon that it demands closer attention. That this insatiable delight in the world of objects is so consistently and universally observed in autistic children, shows it as a necessary step towards the attainment of their full personhood. Indeed, their typical progression in interest from *part* to *whole* object reveals a slow flowering of consciousness as the autistic infant rises through the liminal curtain to meet the world without.

The Pythian child's objects of play can mirror those of their psychotypical peers, but often deviate widely, favouring objects of a highly eccentric nature over toys such as dolls or action figures that would facilitate social interaction. My own choice at four years of age was a car and horse float – no person to drive, no horse to be pulled – the vehicles themselves were my delight, the time for humans had not yet come.

That the choices of autistic children are unusual is not in dispute, but who is doing the choosing? It is the *unconscious itself* whose curiosity chooses the object, reaching out and delighting in the structure and novelty of the material world, each precious piece engendering a self-renewing sense of wonder.

When regarding their relational arc in its entirety, this second stage in Pythian psycho-relational development is rarely cause for alarm. It is often noted that individuals on the autism spectrum, when recalling their earliest memories, tend to recall objects rather than people. In my personal experience, in that of my clients and of the Pythian population in general, recalling the intensity of interest in objects to the almost total exclusion of all else, glows with a kind of sweet nostalgia, and can be truly viewed as a *rite of passage* – the crossover point into the realm of the material world in all its wonder.

The singular attachment that young autistic children have towards material objects is typically explained in academic literature in terms of a possible retreat from the difficulty in understanding the thoughts or feelings of others, or as a response to social confusion, or as a *safe alternative* to the uncertainties of human interaction, or that objects and machinery are easier to understand. Granted, the objective world certainly does have the utility of providing the autistic child with a *fall back* from the confusion of the social realm, however, such conjecture falls far short of the truth of the matter, for its origins are not to be found in terms of *escape*, but in an experience of consciousness so delicate, so subtle, as to be out of the range of psychotypical perception. What the Pythian child's love of objects reveals is their sensitivity to the low levels of consciousness that permeate all matter, to which they can readily and passionately relate.

The whole material universe lies along a sliding scale of consciousness from its most simple to its most complex forms: from say, that of a stone, to the full flowering of human consciousness, and the trajectory of Pythiism's relational arc mirrors this ascent. What Pythiism reveals to us at this second level is that the emerging consciousness of the autistic child resonates with the consciousness within matter, and that their being allowed to freely partake in this developmental milestone is absolutely necessary for the good of their psycho-relational development. In other words, let them play with and line up their precious objects for as long as they like, and do not stop them, for their individual and collective development depends upon it!

This understanding of the nature of consciousness as it applies to the material world is, of course, nothing new. The 13th century German theologian, philosopher and mystic Meister Eckhart, in his second sermon eloquently explored the nature of objects. I have paraphrased it as follows: *As certain as I live, there bides nothing so near to me as God. God bides nearer to me than I do to myself; my existence depends upon his abiding presence. He bides too with things of wood and stone, but they know it not. Were a piece of wood to apprehend the nearness of God as does an archangel, that piece of wood would indeed be as happy as an archangel. By this reasoning a human being is happier than inanimate wood, for they know and understand that God is near them.*

The young Pythian child perfectly embodies this metaphysical wisdom, requiring for their good, at this second stage, to relate to *objects* over *people*. I dare say that the autistic child left to play with his or her precious possession is indeed as happy as an archangel, caught up in a kind of ecstasy, enraptured by the object they possess, because they intuit the presence of the divine within it and witness to God's sustaining presence on its behalf. Put quite simply, the child on the autism spectrum is a true contemplative, a natural born mystic.

Such is their degree of admiration for their precious objects, that some young children on the spectrum are apt to *take on* the characteristics of the object itself, deriving hours of pleasure impersonating the rhythmic hum of a washing machine, a dripping tap, a bouncing ball, or the ringtone of a telephone to the exclusion of their practical and social contexts. This penchant for mimicry too is a pure act of contemplation, rejoicing in the *actuality* of the object, just as it is.

What it all comes down to quite simply, is are we prepared to allow the Pythian child, notwithstanding exposure to social occasions, to spend long stretches of time abiding in their own world where others cannot come, to line up objects over and over again, to fixate on their precious possessions, and to allow all these things – for years – to take precedence over their ability to relate to other people?

My answer to this question is a resounding yes. Why? Because I myself was allowed to do just that, to maintain my personal relationship with the world of matter, and to emerge at my own pace and in my own time, ultimately to my great and lasting benefit.

It is salutary to recall the Pythia of Delphi being consulted despite the omens being ill-favoured. To pull the Pythian child away from their relationship to objects may not end in their demise, but it will certainly have the potential to disrupt their smooth progression along their relational arc.

This sensitivity to and relationship with the world of matter that both children and adults on the autism spectrum possess is not without its disconcertions, particularly in terms of body boundary, creating confusion as to the perception of where one's body finishes and an object begins. In the process of making contact with the physical world, the unconscious can occasionally overshoot its boundary, attaching itself to a material object, creating an artefact of consciousness whereby an individual on the autism spectrum is unable to distinguish the demarcation between self and say, a utensil, or the chair on which they sit. This phenomenon, *sticky consciousness* is often but not always exacerbated by stress, and although disconcerting, is in no way harmful, for the oscillation between the unconscious and conscious mind has a wonderful way of recalibrating in real-time.

Once the Pythian child's relationship to objects has been firmly established and thoroughly explored, they are ready to continue rising along the relational arc to that of their relationship to and legendary affinity with the world of animals and nature, which we shall now explore.

Relationship to animals and nature (empathy)

The third level of Pythian psycho-relational development marks the beginning of their transition towards full consciousness, the individual becoming aware for the first time of the happenings around them and their relationship to others. They now begin to turn their attention to flora and fauna, and the rising spectrum of higher consciousness within these living things.

Animals in general and pets in particular play a vital role in providing those on the autism spectrum with consistent companionship and unconditional acceptance in a world where the breaking of social conventions can leave many feeling on the outer. Even so, the legendary and mutual empathy that exists between those on the autism spectrum and the animal kingdom is shaped by factors far more fundamental in nature than that of simple companionship.

Unlike the lower levels of consciousness within the animal kingdom for whom evolution has decreed thus far and no further, the Pythias' alternative form of consciousness has, in an exception to the rule, produced an alchemic fusion of unconscious and conscious awareness, allowing the individual on the spectrum to abide in the anxious wordless world of creatures, to resonate with their vulnerabilities, to intuit their joys, and it is this that constitutes their mysterious empathetic bond.

Conversely, pets pick up on the sorrows and anxieties of their Pythian owners, giving rise to the training of emotional support animals (ESAs) that provide both companionship and safety, their constant presence calming and reassuring both children and adults, and reducing their overall stress. Wherever there are people on the autism spectrum, there animals will be: a phenomenon I call the Saint Francis Effect. The empathy emanating from their place within the unconscious constitutes, for those on the autism spectrum, a genuine *fellow feeling* that informs their readiness to soothe and understand the world of nature on its own terms.

Many people on the autism spectrum display a singular sensitivity to the joys and anxieties of plant-life, such as witnessing the exuberance in a row of palm trees on a windy day or the fatigue of a pot plant in need of water or a kind word. Again, the delicacy of Pythian perception comes from their awareness of the low levels of consciousness within the botanical world, and it is this quality of perception that is at the heart of their sense of stewardship for the earth.

The Pythia attend to the lives of not only the most complex, but also the smallest and most vulnerable of species, not as dispassionate observers, but in relationship with everything that meets their eye and ear and touch, and it is from their *shared place* within the unconscious that so many on the autism spectrum advocate for the environment, that is, *speak on its behalf.*

Just as the Pythia of Delphi held laurel leaves in one hand, and a shallow dish of spring water into which she gazed in the other, so do those on the autism spectrum turn their full attention to the plight of the environment: its forests, rivers, soil and atmosphere on which animals and people alike depend, pronouncing passionately – seemingly more than human – prophecies of the future, warning of environmental catastrophes and their effects on the delicate ecosystems of our planet.

Not content with mere words, the Pythia are quick to contribute their talents and resources to furthering the well-being of fauna and flora of all kinds, and are well represented among entomologists, botanists, zoologists, environmental officers, vets, national park rangers, volunteers in animal shelters, wildlife rescue workers and various other professions that serve the needs of animals and their environment.

Their empathetic relationship to the world of nature and animal life is folded into their way of being and they are ready to continue their ascent to the most crucial and definitive level of their psycho-relational development, that of their relationship to and compassion for the world of other people.

Relationship to people (compassion)

The fourth level of Pythian psycho-relational development is often characterised by the degree of turbulence they encounter as they rise from the unconscious to meet and understand the world of other people. Swapping out symbols for logic, the individual learns over many years the language and culture of a land that, at first foreign, can become truly their own.

As such, the social confusion universally experienced by young children on the autism spectrum can be understood in relation to their traversing over and over again the threshold between the unconscious and conscious realms. This continual oscillation necessitates the need to seek the path of least resistance, the effects of which can be plainly seen in the abrupt, direct and unvarnished communication inspired by the unconscious mind *out of its depth*, employing logic as a coping mechanism, generating the sort of scenario that has the Pythian child skip up to a potential playmate and proudly declare "the square root of 81 is 9". The fragmented lessons learned in the conscious realm are slowly, painstakingly and often painfully pieced together over many years, building up at length a general picture of the social terrain.

The challenges the Pythia have in creating social connections with the psychotypical population are not, of course, limited to social awareness. They display in every encounter all their modes of operating: unusual language and cognition, anxiety, anger and guilt, culturally unusual and highly focused interests, sensory sensitivity, struggles with motor movement and coordination and unnerving psychic perception, signalling a gulf between themselves and those whom they encounter. Nevertheless, it is these same qualities that create an unbreakable bond between them and their fellow human beings, whether on or off the spectrum, which we will continue to explore throughout this work.

Just as the Pythia of Delphi could only be consulted one day a month, the effort of the consultations leaving her shaking and spent with exhaustion, so do the Pythia, despite their desire to interact with others, suffer social exhaustion on a daily basis, requiring extended times of solitude to decompress after engaging with psychotypical people, by being alone. In the time of the oracles, the purpose of the Pythia of Delphi's sacred selection was steeped in a call to Being, becoming, as it were, an ambassador representing all the peoples of the ancient world, to dwell in solitude between the place of gods and men on their behalf.

What is evident to anyone who pays close attention to Pythian Being, is that it is marked by a most profound personal solitude. No matter how many surround them, even when socially engaged, they seem essentially, alone. However, the *solitude* of the Pythian individual is in direct counter balance to the *multitude* of lives whose experience is laid down in the collective unconscious, to which the Pythia, seated in the unconscious, have access. The Pythian relationship to the experience of generations that have gone before them is once again expressed as a ratio of one-to-many.

On their way to full maturity, the Pythia must endure, over many years, a most sustained and courageous act of becoming. The mechanism by which the individual can continue to progress along the path of psycho-relational development, is by bridging the chasm between themselves and others, and that bridge is Being itself.

As such, this crucial stage of their psycho-relational development is marked not only by the turbulence they experience in rising to find their place among other people, but also by the sheer joy of human encounter. Their entry point into full consciousness comes not through *conversation* but through *contemplation*.

And herein lies the essence of what it means for the Pythia to finally arrive at their highest form of relationship: to experience within themselves the full flowering of human consciousness by means of a single oscillation rising through the liminal curtain – in a single moment, they lock onto the apprehension of the simple beauty of another human being, causing the Pythian individual to live out of that flash of contemplative inspiration for the rest of their life.

Now that is not to say that every human being with which one comes into contact will readily manifest this *simple beauty* of which I speak. We have all lived long enough and suffered enough at the hands of others to show caution where it is due. Nevertheless, the contemplative perspective to which the Pythia are naturally inclined, not only enables them to recognise the unique beauty and dignity of another human being – which only another human being is capable of apprehending – but also introduces the possibility of recovering from the suffering caused by other people.

Yes, the Pythia have their sufferings, and it is these very sufferings that can become a bridge of compassion (Latin *com-passion* – to suffer with) between themselves and others.

In doing so, they reach out to others from the depths of their strengths and limitations like their namesake the Pythia of Delphi, interceding between the place of gods and men, serving as sentinels of *universal compassion*; and it is this disposition that enables them to connect with others, psychotypical or not, equipped as they are to shoulder not only the burden of the sufferings of other people, but also to gracefully shoulder their own.

The Pythian individual endures a lifelong creative tension pitched between the unconscious and conscious spheres of influence whose relational trajectory has been defined by that of constant ascent. Each level of relationship – whether it be a fleeting image, a treasured teacup, a precious pet, or a special friend – each fully lived, is folded into an integrated whole, and the Pythian individual now prepares for their final oscillation, descending into the mystery from which they first sprung.

Relationship to the collective unconscious: descending (surrender)

The fifth and final level of Pythian psycho-relational development marks a turning point, a descent, drawing the now ageing Pythian at length into the realm of those who have gone before them.

The unconscious, which has willingly shared and delighted in the conscious experience of the Pythian individual, now begins to beckon, drawing them quite literally, in their *declining years* into their inner-world again, where each makes their solitary journey alone. This turning of their attention signals a gradual *letting go*, a quietening of the mind and a general withdrawal perceptible to those who know them best. There is a corresponding increase in the need to *vocalise* their way through process, to pay more attention to detail, to plan in advance, in short, to tether themselves to a receding connection to the conscious world.

The Pythia come into this world acutely aware of the mystery that surrounds them. With curiosity, wonder, empathy, and compassion satisfied and the oscillations of a lifetime stilled in death, they surrender to the mystery from which they first sprang, and laying down their life experience, they enrich the wisdom of the collective unconscious below.

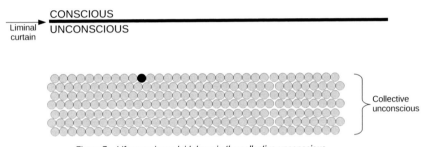

Figure 7 – Life experience laid down in the collective unconscious

CHAPTER 7

Pythia and her passions

(special interests)

The special interests of those on the autism spectrum are without doubt the most celebrated aspect of their nature; from the sublime to the ridiculous and everything in between, there is barely a subject or object that cannot become an all-consuming Pythian passion.

However, despite constant exposure, Pythian individuals remain strangely impervious to the pastimes and common interests of their own culture, their preferred interests often flying in the face of those of their psychotypical peers. Given their social challenges and their desire for friendship and connection, with so readily accessible a framework of sport, fashion and streaming services to grease the wheels of social interaction, why would they choose otherwise?

Quite simply, when it comes to their special interests, it is *the unconscious* that does the choosing. The unconscious delights in its access to the conscious realm, picking and choosing with all the unbounded enthusiasm and energy at its disposal that which appeals to it, sometimes for a short time, sometimes for a lifetime.

That the unconscious is in the driving seat when it comes to choice more than explains the obscurity, indeed, oddity of many of the interests Pythian individuals have been known to take up, whether it be a treasured collection of bottle tops, or an encyclopaedic knowledge of the celestial hierarchy.

The Pythian collector, too, has a distinct point of departure from the psychotypical enthusiast, filling not just a few display cabinets or shelves with their prized possessions, but room upon room, loft to basement, each piece lovingly catalogued and cared for. In keeping with their unique sensitivity to objects, they will spend many hours of their leisure time communing with their collections. Seated in the unconscious, they retreat more deeply into their inner-scape to enjoy and examine their treasures procured from the world without.

Moreover, rather than acquiring a large variety of precious pieces, the Pythia have a distinct propensity for collecting items of the same genre: glass bottles, dolls, match-boxes, model trains, clocks, action figures and the like – a single theme endlessly pursued.

What can possibly generate this inexhaustible zeal for repetition? Each and every time the ascending oscillation passes through the liminal curtain into consciousness, the Pythian mind receives that which is presented to it as perpetually novel.

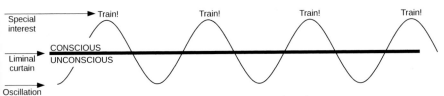

Figure 8 – Oscillation producing perpetual novelty

The ascending oscillation rises again and again into consciousness, transforming what is classified in the DSM-5 as restrictive, repetitive behaviour, into a self-renewing sense of wonder. This knowledge in turn unlocks our understanding of many Pythian passions, such as the delight young children on the autism spectrum have in lining up objects – the pleasure and novelty in each placed piece, or their love of spinning objects whose rotations are an eternal round of perfection sympathetic to the oscillations of their mind.

Those on the spectrum will eagerly focus for hours on one

thing without a moment's boredom and will enjoy listening to a song or piece of music over and over again without fatigue. They will happily eat the same food, meal after meal, relishing the same taste and texture day in, day out – and all because of the nature of their alternative form of consciousness, its oscillations continually springing fresh into the conscious mind. For them, there is no such thing as monotony.

When it comes to self-expression, far from being a shrinking violet, the unconscious delights in expressing itself, as can be witnessed in much of the artwork produced by those on the autism spectrum. With themes surreal, its moods have a dream-like, subliminal quality, rich in symbolism, drawn from palettes as dark and as florid as the fragmented images that rise in the hours of sleep, giving what is unconscious a voice.

Conversely, the art of those seated most deeply in the unconscious takes on a far more literal quality, with images matching language at a ratio of one-to-one, whose literal interpretation acts as a grappling hook, using precision to anchor itself in the conscious realm.

What is more, the unconscious has a sense of style – as long as it comes in black! It is not that the Pythian individual is incapable of enjoying coloured fabrics, or avoids having to make a choice; rather, black – the preferred shade of so many on the spectrum – is the colour of their native land – their *national costume* woven from the dark recesses of the unconscious in which they live and move and have their being, grounding them, and giving full expression to subliminal style.

The interests to which the Pythian population are drawn have a universal quality, transcending both nationality and culture, consistently springing up among them regardless of their country of origin. By contrast the interests of psychotypical people – whose perception is largely bound to conscious life – tend to be generational and of their time, regional and contextual, and therefore short-lived; whereas the

Pythia – seated in the unconscious – draw their interests from the collective unconscious below – taking up the interests and attitudes of previous generations as though they were their very own, gaining them the title of Old Souls.

Many Pythian interests fall under both ancient and nostalgic themes: think fossils and dinosaurs, medieval fairs, Victorian fashion, old telephones, and the ubiquitous train spotter whose encyclopaedic knowledge includes disbanded Victorian railways: their stations, routes and staff, and antiques: artefacts that to Pythian perception resonate with the lives of those who have – just this moment – set them aside.

Here there is a fundamental principal at play: the unconscious preferring old to new, ancient to modern. The Pythia intuit the collective experience of times long past still effervescing in the shallows of the unconscious, influencing their pastimes, passions and tastes, their sense of nostalgia felt on behalf of the lives of those who have preceded them.

However noteworthy in itself, to where does this propensity for the past ultimately point? By virtue of their alternative form of consciousness, the Pythia are custodians of Deep Time: a perception of the unbroken thread of human becoming on whose psycho-evolutionary continuum each individual and generation sits, each one singularly and collectively adding to the lifting of consciousness from one generation to the next.

Their custodial role for deep time manifests not only in their chosen interests, but also in their preoccupation with eras, dates and timelines, and their making connections between contemporaneous lives across many generations – rejoicing in the interwoven fabric of human endeavour.

Seated just below the liminal curtain, the Pythia pivot between two points: that of yearning for the distant past and eagerly anticipating an unknown future. Their special interests, whether they be historic or futuristic, echo the Pythia's privileged role: giving thanks for humanity's uninterrupted psycho-evolutionary journey through time and space.

CHAPTER 8

Pythia's partial view

(sensory sensitivity)

To fully understand the phenomena of sensory sensitivity synonymous with those on the autism spectrum, we need to begin with a fundamental assertion: the unconscious is blind. The unconscious does not see but rather, intuits the conscious world. The Pythia of Delphi descended alone into the darkness of the Adyton, the deepest and most inaccessible room within the temple. Likewise, to be seated within the realm of the unconscious is to experience the physical world as though by night. The Pythia *feel* their way around their five senses: sight, hearing, smell, touch and taste, running their fingers around the contours of the sensory world.

What is known about those on the spectrum in relation to their marked sensory sensitivities, is that nothing in their sensory faculties has been pinpointed to suggest that they are compromised or especially enabled in any way, and so the questions persist: why are sounds so loud, smells so pungent, tastes so overpowering, textures so off-putting, visuals so confusing, and why does such adverse stimulation assail the Pythia all at once?

The Pythia are seated in the unconscious, and as such, they perceive the sensory world from a point far below the surface of the conscious mind. It is this tyranny of distance that accounts for the sensory distortions to which they are prone. The Pythia, by dint of the oscillation between their unconscious and conscious mind, have been given a *partial view* through the liminal curtain, through which they constantly catch sight of the world without.

Their extended gestational period in early life, in which the connecting oscillation between the unconscious and conscious mind is at its most fragile, accounts for the heightened degree of sensory sensitivity to which Pythian children are particularly prone. The sensory information gathered from the surface breaks down and becomes distorted as the descending oscillation carries it further and further away from the point of first contact, faltering and failing to convey the original message, finally delivering it corrupted into the unconscious mind. So it is that a hug can feel claustrophobic, the ring of a phone violent, a hand-knitted jumper penitential, the texture of some foods repulsive, a perfume nauseating, a colour confronting and light unbearable.

In regard to their sensory experiences filtered through their unconscious perception, the Pythia are *unsighted* by nature, and therefore maintain a hyper-vigilance as they feel their way around the physical world, interpreting and often misinterpreting that which presents to their senses. So it is that they can and often do feel threatened by sensory experiences, appraising all with which they come into physical contact with a great deal of caution.

In the rare vigilance observed in those on the spectrum, we see that each and every time the ascending oscillation passes through the liminal curtain into consciousness, the mind receives that which is presented to it as perpetually novel. It is this perception, unique among the Pythia, that is responsible for them having difficulty adjusting to new stimuli no matter how many times a day or how frequent the exposure. This is why they can go about their day in an almost constant state of shock and surprise. Indeed, they can still get a shock even when they know the surprise is coming. How is this so? It is because the Pythian mind is always springing afresh into conscious awareness, and it is this that fuels their fear of the unexpected.

This propensity for finding surprises unpleasant is also heightened by their tendency to *power down*, taking their seat in the unconscious more firmly when not otherwise occupied, which only magnifies the startle effect to which they are prone. It is no wonder that the random explosion of a bursting balloon at a birthday party is rated number one in the nerve-shattering stimuli to which they can be exposed.

Let us turn our attention to another category of sound sensitivity: sounds of a high-pitched, continuous quality, including those emitted from domestic appliances such as vacuum cleaners, food processors, or the sound of a flushing toilet, these being universally documented as extremely aversive in the autobiographies of those on the autism spectrum. Be that as it may, it is not the high pitch of the appliances themselves on which our focus of attention should be trained, but why the Pythian perception of high-pitched sounds should have such an adverse effect at all.

The levels of discomfort they experience with high-pitched sounds are due to their direct effect upon the oscillation between the unconscious and conscious mind. What links the two is that they both share a high-pitched continuous frequency, which although not in any way harmful to the individual, nevertheless can cause a disturbance to their sense of equilibrium. The effect can be likened to the static produced on a radio when two stations are competing to use the same frequency: in this case, one frequency is produced by sound waves, the other by waves of psychic energy, creating a *white noise* which causes distress. As soon as the interference of the high-pitched appliance is removed, for them, normal programming can resume.

The final category of sound sensitivity is for sounds that are multilayered and simultaneous in nature, such as is generated in shopping centres and noisy social settings, the effects of which assail the Pythian perception as a cacophony of garbled and chaotic noise. This can cause confusion and mental exhaustion in the Pythian individual, whose oscillating perception desperately tries to pinpoint the detail in a jumble of conflicting sounds. This type of sensory confusion often manifests in a general sense of disorientation. Removing themselves from the confronting environment allows their equilibrium to be restored.

The Pythia's discomfort around competing stimulation is also observed in their sense of taste, seen in their propensity to separate the items of food on their dinner plate into like groups: for example, one space for peas, another for carrots, yet another for potatoes, as well as for meat – borders worthy of a cluster of small European nations – and once satisfied that none is encroaching on the boundary of another, they will set about methodically consuming each separate type of food, allowing the ascending oscillation to hone in on simple detail, avoiding confusion from the mixing of texture and taste. The mashing and combining of the contents of food on their plates to which the psychotypical population are given remains, from a sensory point of view for the Pythia, an anathema.

The unconscious is a poor interpreter of the physical world, and the tyranny of distance between it and the world of conscious experience continues to distort the Pythias' sense of taste, texture and smell. Indeed the Pythias' hypersensitivity to the smell and texture of many foods is, in essence, an artefact of the unconscious' own struggle to understand input which is outside of its lived experience. This accounts for why many Pythian children and some adults insist on bland, uncomplicated food such as bread, noodles and pancakes, anything that takes the strain off the unconscious' interpretation of their sensory experience.

Certain visual cues can also adversely affect the Pythia, for example, those induced by over-busy patterns in carpet, or conversely, exposure to large areas of indeterminate colours such as walls painted in pastel colours or plain white. In the intricate patterns of a carpet, the problem for the Pythia is that there is too much information for the ascending oscillation to process; in the case of pastel or white walls, there is too little: both confirm the way in which the ascending oscillation proceeding from the unconscious requires a solid, clear and unadulterated signal on which to latch in order to adequately interpret the sensory world.

This way of looking at the sensory processing of the Pythia also explains why, when it comes to physical contact, they prefer firm pressure to a light touch, working on a simple and effective premise: the better the contact, the better the signal transmitted to the unconscious mind.

The effects of hyper- and hyposensitivity in Pythian individuals can be seen in matters as endearingly straightforward as in the case of one lady I knew who smothered everything she ate in hot chilli sauce, giving her the strong connection she required to taste her food. Another I knew had a preference for food that was as bland as the day is long: white bread, milk and plain boiled potatoes, signalling the over-stimulation of her senses to which she was prone; others see-saw between the spicy and the insipid, hot and cold, quiet and loud, resonating with their inner oscillation.

The psychic energy that oscillates between the unconscious and conscious mind waxes and wanes as all energy does, and it is this tendency that is responsible for the *tune outs* to which the Pythia are prone. That the Pythian individual can experience a temporary and fluctuating loss of perception, even when concentrating on what someone is saying, affirms that they are not having a *lapse in concentration* nor *not attending to what is being said*, but are genuinely and literally *losing the thread* of conversation – the thread being the oscillation which links unconscious and conscious perception, petering out with the resultant loss of auditory information.

For those on the spectrum there is an almost complete inability to read the signs of what would register to most psychotypicals as physical discomfort: the mothers of Pythian children following them around in the dead of winter, imploring them to put on a nice warm jumper when their child insists that they aren't cold in their shorts and t-shirt, or having to witness their child's insistence on wearing long trousers at the height of summer.

The oscillation that weaves its way between Pythiism's two worlds also generates sensory delights. The self-renewing novelty that the ascending oscillation produces, becomes a springboard for many of the simple pleasures that come under the umbrella of obsessive behaviour in children on the spectrum, such as repeatedly ringing a doorbell, or continually turning a light switch on and off, simply for the thrill of the feel and sound.

This pleasure not only applies to sounds, but also to sights, odours, textures and flavours, through which the Pythia not only appraise the physical world, but through which they are also captivated by its beauty. Some examples from my own and others' sensory experiences that are pure pleasure include: the sound of drinking glasses thrumming on contact, a spinning coin on a hard surface, the thunk of the ticking of a grandfather clock, and my personal favourite, the sound of a single mosquito whose resonant whine on a still night shares the harmonic and discordant qualities of Gregorian chant.

The Pythia's sensory sensitivity is not only an intermittent source of passing pleasure, but also provides for many a solid foundation on which to build their careers. Thus can a Pythian's exquisitely discerning palate find them hidden away in the cool dark cellars of famous vineyards appraising vintage wines, or starting a micro-brewery whose beer rivals the centuries-old recipes brewed behind monastic walls; or using their subtle sense of smell to skilfully blend the notes for designer fragrances; or their eye for colour and feel for fabric to design for top fashion houses, their creations veritable works of art.

As the oscillation between the unconscious and conscious mind strengthens into adulthood, for some, there is a corresponding reduction in distress caused by environmental triggers. Furthermore, it is a wonderful thing to note that as the most pronounced of their sensory sensitivities fall away, their finely tuned capacity for pleasure in the subtle, almost hidden sensory experiences of nature, remain not only intact, but strengthen and refine as a lasting legacy in their relationship with the sensory world.

CHAPTER 9

Pythia enthroned in the temple

(motor movement and coordination)

When we apply Pythiism's principal of personhood seated in the unconscious we soon arrive at a platform for exploring the difficulties and impediments associated with motor-movement and coordination within this population that is far more open to interpretation than what is usually considered. The interplay between the psyche and movement expressed by those on the autism spectrum once again affirms that it is the unconscious that shapes matter and not the other way around, the ramifications of which shall now be explored.

The Pythia of Delphi descended into the deepest and most inaccessible room within the temple, mounting her tripod seat and clinging for support to nothing except the laurel leaves in her trembling hand, and so it is for the those on the autism spectrum. To be enthroned in the temple of the unconscious is to be permitted to dwell as deeply within its reaches as possible, and yet still have the capacity – no matter how tentative – to maintain a grasp on the physical world.

In this way, the Pythia maintain a bridge between their physical and unconscious selves, and the difficulties that they experience in maintaining their connection with the physical world can be understood in a new light: that their idiosyncratic ungainly movements are no longer markers of mere clumsiness, but are indicative of the dignity of their uniquely privileged position within the unconscious.

Difficulties with motor movement may not be unique to Pythiism, but its origin is. That it is a matter of the struggle to achieve coordination is a given, but it is a struggle to achieve coordination in a far more fundamental sense – that of the unconscious and conscious mind working together to maintain equilibrium across two states of being: one predominantly psychic, the other, physical.

The poor core strength and low muscle tone associated with autism is a principal feature of the condition, but what can that tell us of the unconscious in which such symptoms originate? This too can be interpreted as a consequence of Pythiism's alternative form of consciousness whose primary position creates the necessity to conserve energy deep within the unconscious to serve its greater need.

This primordial posture and conservation of psychic energy comes at great cost to the individual, compelled as they are by the continual counter-balance of having to rise precipitously from the depths of the unconscious in which they are seated to meet the world without; not once, but perennially.

The Pythia function primarily through their unconscious mind. That the unconscious dictates motor movement and coordination within this population can be witnessed in their first faltering steps. One of the first markers of autism in movement, particularly in those seated most deeply within the unconscious mind, is their propensity to walk on the tips of their toes, as if in wry recognition of their tentative connection with the physical world.

What begins for many as a slight delay in the ability to walk in infancy, continues to be manifested over their developmental milestones and into adulthood through disturbances of gross-motor movement observed in unusual gait in both walking and running locomotion, poor posture, poor limb coordination, lack of ball skills and balance. For many, their physical experience is one of feeling *fundamentally ungrounded*.

For certain Pythian individuals, motor coordination disintegrates the moment they are required to think. For them, the amount of energy required to process thought requires them to martial their psychic resources, which in turn creates a corresponding cessation of physical movement; reanimating, as it were, once the process of thought is completed, redistributing once more that energy which is required to assist the body.

Their need to withdraw to conserve their psychic energy reflects that experienced by the Pythia of Delphi, whose sessions within the temple left her shaking and spent with exhaustion like a marathon runner, or a dancer after a frenzied dance. It can hardly be overstated that many individuals on the autism spectrum are brought not only to the brink of mental exhaustion, but also physical exhaustion on a daily basis.

The variances Pythian children display in orientating themselves in the physical world confirm the relative strength of the ascending or descending oscillation. A weaker ascending oscillation, rising from the seat of the unconscious, will pass through the liminal threshold perceiving motor-movement as a sensory overload, manifesting in extreme anxiety on their feet leaving the ground, such as when being picked up and carried or turned upside-down; severing the awareness of what little physical connection the unconscious was able to grasp; this is evident in that placing a young Pythian child on the seat of a swing may be enough to send them into a panic, such is their need to feel grounded.

Conversely, a stronger descending oscillation, carrying information from the world of motor-movement to that of the seat of the unconscious, will manifest in a strong preference for seeking and enjoying movement, such as trampolining, swings and roundabouts, climbing and fairground rides, with a corresponding physical facility for sport and gymnastic type activities, born of a firm signal being conveyed back to the unconscious mind. Over time the ascending and descending oscillations strengthen and stabilise, ensuring a basic physical stability with age, equilibrium.

Other manifestations of the unconscious in motor movement, particularly evident in early childhood, fall into the category of self-stimulatory behaviours – such as rocking, humming, hand flapping, tapping, twirling, drumming one's fingers or jiggling one's leg. These are typically expressed for one of two reasons: to soothe oneself when feeling overwhelmed by sensory or emotional triggers, or for the sheer joy and pleasure to be had by partaking in repetitive movements. Such repetitions resonate with the oscillation produced between the unconscious and conscious mind, creating and confirming a sense of harmony between their two states of being.

The unconscious, too, leaves its signature in their handwriting. The propensity for their writing style to chop and change wildly, even in the course of writing a single word, uncovers the effects of the oscillation that resets their writing style from one moment to the next: now cursive, now printed, now capitals, now lower case – confirming that the lack of consistency so evident in the written word of so many, is an artefact produced by the oscillation between the unconscious and conscious mind. The dominance of the unconscious mind, too, often asserts itself in their style of handwriting, executing highfalutin flourishes peculiar to the individual, trumping what was originally taught.

It is satisfying to see the intuitive way in which occupational therapy has developed over the years to serve their physical needs, employing strategies such as the use of weighted blankets, weighted lap pillows and pencils – dialling up the volume on the physical world – as well as activities like stamp-walking and jumping to help the client make good contact between their body and the ground on which they walk. All these measures speak of the practical instinct for this alternative form of consciousness, whose sense of balance is served by promoting the connection between their two forms of functioning – the psychic and the physical.

Much is written of their awkwardness, but the exception proves the rule: some possess a gracefulness of movement and gesture that is both subtle and elegant. Among them are runway and magazine models, dancers and acrobats, actors and athletes, and performers in every known discipline. For them, the robust connection between their inner and outer worlds becomes a springboard, enabling them to take their place in society in a highly physical forum.

Related to their expression of motor movement is their need for routine. For them, establishing daily and often rigid routines, from the way they make their morning coffee, to route they drive to work, or the order in which they eat their lunch, is intimately linked to the disorientation experienced on emerging time and again into the conscious mind.

This perpetual rising into consciousness creates a low-grade disorientation that is attenuated by establishing certain daily patterns of behaviour – scaffolding their conscious experience by way of a running commentary of self-instruction: "now I do this, now I do that". Such scaffolding acts as a compass, orienting them in the physical world, much in the same way a physically blind person orders their environment to suit, for the unconscious is unsighted by nature.

Notwithstanding the ungainliness almost universal in the Pythian population, there is one aspect of their physicality that has not ceded to rule: that of the symmetry of the face. There does the unconscious most perfectly reflect its nature, leaving its signature: an imprint of exquisite and preternatural beauty, whose impress is a veronica (Latin *vera-icon* – true image) of the unconscious, bending matter to its will.

In essence, their relationship to the physical world can be likened to that of a tightrope walker under the Big Top: poised, graceful, arms outstretched, employing all their skill as they make their way, one trembling foot in front of the other, to reach the far side. The crowd do not see their knocks and bruises, nor are they privy to the multitude of falls that it took for them to be able to perform. A high-wire act on terra firma, the descending Pythian smiles and takes their bow, disappearing behind the liminal curtain into the shadows once more to rapturous applause.

CHAPTER 10

Pythia and her prophecies

(psychic phenomena and spirituality)

It is often thought that individuals on the autism spectrum lack the capacity for symbolic expression – a necessary disposition for the comprehension of the spiritual and certainly the religious realm. However, for the sake of communication in the conscious world and its inherent difficulty, for many, symbolic expression is necessarily tempered if not seemingly quarantined at the point of liminal exchange.

Despite their heavy leaning towards logic, nevertheless the supernatural is continually breaking through. Even for those on the spectrum who purport to be neither spiritual nor religious, their presentation belies a sensitivity to the supernatural that is evident to the observer – radiating a psychic energy that is a manifestation of the unconscious itself. The archetype of the Pythia of Delphi echoes the experience of those on the autism spectrum. They are chosen from among many to fulfil a prophetic role, one filled with dignity and honour, wonder and mystery.

For them, there exists the thinnest membrane between the unconscious and conscious mind. Inaccessible to most, from within their unconscious waking awareness emanates the rich and symbolic material produced by the unconscious nearing its upper reaches, the place where dreams and the surreal are fashioned.

The degree of awareness that the Pythia have in regards to their unconscious mind varies from one to another. I propose that this sliding scale of awareness is in direct proportion to each individual's level of liminal transparency; that is, the extent to which they are able to detect the workings of their unconscious mind.

This seems to account for the degree to which any given person on the spectrum shows inclination towards both the psychic and spiritual life. The greater the transparency, the more they are lifted out of the constraints of the conscious world.

Given their unprecedented access to the unconscious – being seated within it – for some, it is not so much that they *believe* in the supernatural realm, but that they are *assailed* by it. The fertile and florid symbols within the unconscious, which are its native language, bubble up into conscious awareness: a self-renewing spring of psychic phenomena and imagery to enthral, fascinate and captivate their curiosity and attention, manifesting in symbolic dreams and waking visions, taking on a life of their own.

Their sensitivity towards both the personal and collective unconscious commonly manifests in extrasensory perception, such as the palpable awareness of the hidden sufferings of others both living and dead, the seeing of ghosts and the activity of poltergeists, premonitions and the reception of information regarding another that one could not possibly know, and other manifestations of the paranormal.

These modes of psychic perception, although not exclusive to them, nevertheless express a range of perceptual function uncommon among the psychotypical population, for over my many years of working with perfectly ordinary individuals on the autism spectrum, they have – with monotonous regularity – related to me quite openly their ongoing and persistent experience of paranormal phenomena.

Given their sensitivity towards the psychic realm, it is not by chance that the liminal curtain plays a primary role in offering protection, providing a buffer from the excesses of their unconscious mind. This intrinsic role of *safeguarding* is crucial in the formation of their alternative form of consciousness, regulating by degrees the transferral of content between their unconscious and conscious perception.

Be that as it may, whether child or adult, they present as an archetypal Alice in Wonderland: whatever they eat, whatever they drink, whomever they meet becomes a risky undertaking with no certain outcome. Alice lived the Wonderland experience in her sleep: the Pythian population live it during their waking hours. Interfacing with the unconscious, they find themselves perennially falling down the rabbit hole, from whence who knows what will emerge?

The delicate thread of psychic energy, tenuous and fragile, which oscillates between their two states of mind, renders the demarcation between their unconscious and conscious selves in early childhood of paper-thin permeability. This accounts for the Pythian child's personal anxiety within nocturnal hours as the unconscious breaks through, vividly, into conscious awareness. There are, of course, night-time fears shared with psychotypical children, such as fear of the dark and of monsters: manifestations of the fears of our primitive ancestors whose lives were slung between the dark recesses of the cave and the wild beasts without – fears now smoothed and settled by bedtime routines that usher in the nightly journey into the unconscious for all.

However, the nocturnal fears of Pythian children tend to have a flavour all of their own, such as the fear that items of clothing hung on the back of the door might suddenly fill with personifications from another realm, that a bedroom or wardrobe door left slightly ajar may become a portal through which unknown figures may enter, or shoes casually left on the floor might suddenly and of their own volition, begin to walk across the room.

These and other nightly terrors revolving around personi-fication arise near the time of sleep when the demarcation between the unconscious and conscious mind is at its most permeable, allowing archetypal manifestations of the unconscious to press upon conscious perception. These levels of apprehension can and often do fill the child with a degree of anxiety that is often difficult for a parent to console, let alone understand. In short, the psychotypical child fears what might come from without, whereas the Pythian child fears what might come from within.

This is the point at which ritualistic behaviour kicks in – imposing order where the threat of chaos is perceived: firstly in the hours of night, then quickly followed in the hours of day as the child becomes increasingly aware of the numinous quality of their experience, the gossamer-thin demarcation between their unconscious and conscious mind becoming more apparent.

The Pythia of Delphi's service at the Temple of Apollo was filled with ritual practices: having fasted, the Oracle would purify herself, bathing in the nearby sacred spring and drinking of its holy waters. Processing along the sacred way with her many companions holding laurel branches and incanting sacred poems, she arrived at length at the entrance to the temple where a sacrificial goat would be offered. All these actions had to be fulfilled before the Pythia could enter the temple, whereupon, removing her purple veil, she, clothed in a white garment, would finally descend into the Adyton to receive and proclaim the prophecies.

The adoption of ritualistic behaviour among the autistic population is often viewed, psychologically speaking, as having a pedestrian quality: a utilitarian antidote to a bothersome and anxious turn of mind. However, as noted in the example of the oracular procedures performed throughout the history of the Temple of Apollo, from their inception, human rituals have always and with great earnestness expressed the spiritual life.

The ritualistic behaviour so synonymous with those on the autistic spectrum is not primarily about *controlling anxiety*, but is essentially concerned with expressing a spirituality *in the face of anxiety*, however vague the expression may be. The role of ritual is so much more necessary for those who perennially cross the threshold into their unconscious mind.

Those on the autism spectrum are masters of intuiting what they need in their general environment to thrive, a quality that by necessity extends also to their inner-environment through the adoption of certain ritualistic practices and interests that attend and give expression to their spiritual reality, exampled as follows.

Tattoos – the symbolic material of their unconscious inner-world, rich with archetypal images displayed on the outer – the ethereal images within their unconscious mind made flesh.

Computer games – with archetypal themes and epic quests connecting online players from all over the globe, and online communities whose mind-boggling amounts of discussion threads centre around canon and non-canon interpretations of story arcs and symbols.

Comic conventions – whose devotees arrive by the thousands from across the state and across the globe, reminiscent of the joyful and exuberant medieval pilgrimages of Chaucer's *Canterbury Tales*. Robed in the costume – painstakingly sewn and with no expense spared – of their hero, the wearer is transformed into a superhero lifted from the pages of comic folklore, lifting them for a long-weekend beyond the constraints of the seemingly commonplace and mundane.

Sci-fi and fantasy – whose online communities dedicate themselves to the plots and characters of television cult classics and epic stories such as *Star Trek, Doctor Who, Lord of the Rings, The Hobbit,* and *Harry Potter*. Some devotees make it their life's passion to preserve and hand down the purity of these epic tales, holding television scriptwriters to account with inquisitory zeal for the smallest deviation in the integrity of plots; or memorising the lines of scripts from cult classics with all the fervour once reserved for the recitation of scripture. Some go further still, teaching themselves how to speak Klingon, or to write in the characters of J.R.R. Tolkien's mythical languages in the hope of realising the total immersion of themselves into these sci-fi and fantasy worlds.

It is no secret that the Pythia often endow the archetypes contained within these epic tales of pop-culture with a significance bordering on the religious. This is not to be wondered at, for within these stories of the struggle between light and darkness and conquering one's fears and limitations in a higher cause, are contained the fundamental aspirations of the human condition: the triumph of good over evil, virtue over moral weakness, courage in the face of terrors beyond human reckoning, and resurrection over death: themes whose blockbuster gravitas rely on sources endlessly woven from the rich and ample material drawn from ancient mythology and in particular, the religious traditions of the Judaeo-Christian world, whose archetypal treasures have been buried for safe-keeping within the dark vaults of the collective unconscious itself.

In other words, the pageantry that personally and collectively expresses their epic interests cannot easily be extricated from the individual's search for meaning; and the themes of Western spirituality, no matter how tentatively expressed, provide for many a structure in which to interpret their deepest spiritual longings.

These epic themes and the personal and collective rituals they invoke, alleviate the anxieties of and hold such deep attraction for the Pythian psyche in particular, because they allow the individual to explore their personal history within the framework of a story larger than their own. Indeed ritual binds the past, the present and the future both individually and collectively, enabling the individual to encounter their limited experience not in isolation, but within the epic proportions of the human story – its joys, hopes, setbacks and sufferings embraced and nourished by the collective experience of a *grand narrative.*

The grand narrative of the West, from whose foundations have sprung so many of the great stories of culture, has, over many centuries, proven itself an existential compass large enough and robust enough to hold the two halves of the Pythias' alternative form of consciousness together in creative and life-giving tension, orienting the individual – whole and entire – in *time* and *space* – the two archetypal themes that perennially drive the fantasy and sci-fi genres that engross the imagination of so many.

What frustrates the Pythian individual in the absence of a grand narrative is what can best be described as a *crisis of interpretation*; that is, an inability to ground their personal experiences of psychic and spiritual phenomena in a framework capable of properly evaluating the complexities of both their psychic and spiritual lives – where they meet and their points of departure. This crisis of interpretation not only applies to the individual on the spectrum, but also to society as a whole.

Far from the preserve of purely academic considerations, this crisis of interpretation has real-life consequences, not least within the clinical setting. When confronted with an autistic client's disclosure of seeing ghosts, the activity of poltergeists, the palpable awareness of the personal sufferings of both the living and the dead and other manifestations of the paranormal brought on by their *natural sensitivity* to the supernatural, the therapist – with no evidence pointing to mental illness – can find themselves backed into a corner with little room to move between either carefully ignoring the client's revelations, or feeling compelled to diagnose such psychic material as evidence of a mental disorder.

So it is that such disclosures, born of an alternative form of consciousness, rather than being attributed to the client's psychic predisposition, may be perceived, in the absence of a grand narrative, as the unintelligible utterings of a broken mind. It is sobering to note that some individuals have found themselves admitted to a psychiatric facility based on their psychic sensitivities alone.

If the ritualistic behaviour of the Pythian population is not primarily about *controlling anxiety*, but rather expressing an intrinsic spirituality *in the face of anxiety*, then it behoves us to pay closer attention to these matters where purely psychological interpretation breaks down. When encountering reports of manifestations of the dead, spirits, ghosts, in short, the effervescent nature of psychic phenomena pressing upon their conscious mind, how are we to interpret the numinous quality of Pythian perception with any confidence?

As a person on the spectrum, and having lived for some years the silent life of a contemplative cloistered nun, I would like to offer an interpretation on these matters out of my own personal experience and understanding that not only affirms the florid workings of the Pythian psyche, but also prunes what is necessary in order to give structure and stability to their whole field of psychic perception.

It is not unusual, in the absence of a solid interpretation of psychic phenomena, for a Pythian individual to fall into one of two reactions in response to personal psychic manifestations: that of disorientation, or conversely, intoxication. What is necessary is to distinguish between the realm of psychic phenomena and that of the spiritual to create order where chaos is often perceived.

The unconscious is not "the place of the dead" but an artefact of the living. The contents of the collective unconscious contain the *legacy* rather than the *actuality* of the individual lives of those who have preceded us. In other words, the great majority of personifications that rise from the unconscious mind in dreams are archetypes: an *imprint* of the experience of countless lives, categorised and bundled together to create a composite image which can manifest as man, woman, child or groups of personages – ambassadors from the realm of the collective experience.

The Pythian individual's personal unconscious selectively

draws up the insight it requires from the contents of the collective experience to meet their individual need. So it is that personal manifestations from the collective unconscious are, in the main, avatars of archetypal experiences, shadowy messengers who take a back seat to the message they convey, and not *lives* in themselves.

The genius of the psyche and its phenomena is that it speaks a language all of its own: pictorial and emotional hieroglyphs jettisoned by the dead and drawn up into the personal unconsciousness to be deciphered and examined at will, both there and in the conscious mind.

The spiritual realm ordinarily operates beyond the senses hidden from view, yet is capable of bursting in upon awareness in manifestations both sacred and malevolent, reminding us at intervals that the demarcation between what seems commonplace and what lies beyond is so fine as to be fairly easily apprehended by Pythian psychic perception, perceiving, as it does, the overlapping nature of conscious, unconscious and collective realities.

What can be garnered from the storehouse of human experience that we call the collective unconscious is indeed vast, but still limited; what is received from the realm of the spirit exists within an ever-receding horizon – inexhaustible and infinite. That the spiritual life intersects with psychic phenomena is a remarkable thing, the life of the unconscious providing the footnotes for what is happening beyond the veil of the senses.

But what of the *actual* manifestations of the dead and their sufferings pressing upon Pythian perception to which they are prone, of ghosts, spirits and apparitions, whether in dreams or waking visions; to what end is such a relationship? For the Pythia, the veil between this world and the next is gossamer thin, and the dead know it.

To consider this question I return to my early childhood. My Pythian life, as with all individual lives, can never be viewed in isolation, but rather through the prism of environment, upbringing, temperament, life experience and personal values. At the age of about six or seven years, I remember exploring an old cemetery in the woods of a country estate at which our family were guests. I remember walking from one grave to the next, praying, as I had been taught, for the souls of the dead.

As a child, the grand narrative of the Catholic faith, its prayers, rituals, imagery and sacraments, offered me strange comfort, and a vast framework in which to interpret my lived experience, one that seemed to speak to the two halves of my psyche and the psychic phenomena to which I was prone. My deep sense of connection with and compassion for the dead found an outlet through intercessory prayer, that is, praying on their behalf – my solitary childhood figure a living counterbalance to the multitude of lives that had gone before.

As I write it is an evening in November, the month the Church dedicates to praying for the souls of the dead. I bless myself from a small bowl of Holy Water, I light a candle in the sacred space within my home, I draw my Rosary beads one-by-one through my fingers, methodically vocalising the repetition of its ancient prayers, and at the end pray, "...and lead all souls to Heaven, especially those most in need of thy mercy".

The Pythia stand at the threshold between the present and the past, the material and the spiritual, as sentinels of universal compassion. That they are perennially poised on the tipping point of consciousness, dictates their heightened capacity to intercede not only on behalf of the present generation, but also on behalf of generations past, of whose presence they are so acutely aware. This to me, perfectly answers the question of how we are to relate to the dead – that they may live.

Epilogue

(know thyself)

The first light of Apollo shone through the wooden shutter of her window. Rising from sleep in her solitary dwelling by the woods she saw, outside, the guard assigned to her house. He ground the flaming end of the torch, by which he had kept the night watch of the new moon, into the dirt, thus reducing its embers to dust and ashes.

She felt hunger for the first time, the days of fasting forgotten in the pursuit of the garment that, for weeks now, she had worked upon her loom. Beside it, folded on the table, she reached out to the purple robe once woven by her mother. The Pythia had insisted on taking it with her at the time she had been chosen. This garment, smooth and seamless, would neither scratch nor irritate her skin, her mother being the finest weaver in all of Delphi. She had kept it, along with the matching veil, with great care. Smoothing her hand across the fine fabric, she recalled the times her mother with immense patience taught her to shuttle the thread across her loom, plying fingers that, despite her best efforts, often refused to do her bidding. "Every thread counts", her mother would say smiling, as the pattern painstakingly took shape over many sittings.

Her heart began to pound as she slipped on the dress, her hands shaking as she placed the veil on her head and wrapped its folds about her shoulders. Strapping on her sandals and drawing in one deep breath, she pushed the door of her dwelling open. "It is time", she called to her guard, who with an acknowledgement walked some distance ahead. The first light crept beyond the woods and illuminated the path before her. All she knew was the wet grass under her feet, the crisp air filling her lungs and the play of dappled light through the trees, as small curious birds hopped from branch to branch, drawn by the sound of her steps.

Beyond the clearing, she saw her waiting companions. Gathered in small groups, they laughed and talked in excited whispers, holding hands and swinging their baskets filled with laurel branches freshly picked from the groves by the Sacred Spring.

Of what did they speak? She watched their gestures and the expressions upon their faces, none of which she could read. "How is it?", she said to herself, "that I can understand the language of the divine Apollo whom I can neither see nor hear, and yet not understand my companions who stand in flesh and blood before me? Some mysteries are withheld from my knowledge…"

On seeing the Pythia, a solemn silence fell upon the young women, who lowered their heads as she approached; for within her gaze, it was said, lay the pathos of the underworld upon which they dare not look. Only one came forward to meet her, the only friend of her youth, who on hearing of her elevation to Pythia became her servant, knowing that she alone could quell her fears. While so different from the oracle, the woman understood her like no other and had chosen to remain by her side, all these years, come what may.

She smiled encouragement to her enigmatic friend, and unwrapping the veil about her head, held it before the Pythia to conceal her as she kneeled and began to bathe her arms and face. Scooping up the sparkling water in her cupped hands, the Pythia took a few sips and watched transfixed as the shimmering drops fell like jewels through her fingers into the waters below.

Momentarily, her friend placed her hand upon the Pythia's shoulder, who looked up to notice that her companions had already taken their places at points along the path she was to walk. Aided by the assistance of her companion, for her movements were often unsure, the Pythia rose from the waters of the Sacred Spring.

The ritual procession soothed the trembling that filled her breast, for no matter how many times she walked the Sacred Way, it was as if she were setting out for the very first time. As she walked, the Pythia took her mind off her mounting fears by giving her full attention to the recitation of the sacred poems she loved so well, repeating them over and over again, stressing every syllable in a tone that was unique unto herself.

Having fixed her eyes on the path before her for the whole of its length, she suddenly looked up to see the temple she was about to enter. Despite how many times she had beheld it, it was a sight to which she had never grown accustomed. She stifled a gasp of astonishment as she gazed upon its mighty columns and read once again the maxim uttered by the Pythia of old, now carved into the stone lintel above its lofty entrance: Gnóthi Sautón. "Know thyself," she softly repeated, turning carved words once again into ephemeral breath. For herself, she knew that the only way that she could acquire such knowledge was by being present to the god within.

Her companions stood some way back from the entrance to the temple, shaking their laurel branches, their incantations reaching fever pitch. She turned her face away as the priests sacrificed a young goat. Overwhelmed by the cacophony that followed, she looked longingly into the cool dark sanctuary which lay just beyond the entrance to the temple. The high priest and her companion accompanied the Pythia over the threshold of the temple, leaving the noise and commotion behind, much to her relief.

She quickly slipped off her sandals and felt the cool marble beneath her bare feet. She removed her robe, but always hesitated before removing her veil. Smooth and familiar, it brought her comfort and reassurance, a little shelter for her head against the myriad of sights and sounds that assailed her senses, a diaphanous shield from the prying eyes of pilgrims whose thoughts and emotions hung heavy on her heart should she encounter them upon the way. This cloth she carefully folded herself before entrusting it to her companion, the one person who really understood its value to her.

Lifting her arms she received the white garment, the weight of its thick folds making her aware, perhaps for the first time since that morning, that she was indeed flesh and blood. Bringing her awareness back to her divinely ordained duties as Pythia of the god Apollo, she turned to the priest and enquired in her direct and imperial manner: "What is the question of which the supplicant desires answer?" The priest produced a small scroll of parchment and read the following: "How are my children to live well, when I myself am dead?"

The Pythia asked the priest to repeat the question and vocalising its contents, made the question her own. She looked to the hand of her friend, who poured water into a shallow dish from a pitcher drawn from the Sacred Spring. As she presented the dish, along with a sprig of laurel picked especially for her, her friend, for a moment, looked straight into the eyes that could pierce the depths of Hades itself.

The high priest and her companion took leave of the Pythia and returned to the pavement outside whilst she, now some way into the temple, stood at the entrance that led to the Adyton. Before the entrance hung a large curtain through whose fabric she saw a faint glow. Disappearing behind the edge of the curtain, she found herself on the other side.

Guided by the guttering flames of torches dimly lighting the narrow way, with small faltering steps she descended deeper and deeper along the dark musty passage that seemed to recede and drop away ever further under her feet. All the while she held, in shaking hands, the small dish of water from the Sacred Spring and the laurel leaves, whose green waxy lustre now, so far beyond the light of the sun, took on a dull grey aspect like the flowers said to bloom beyond the twilight of death. "Fear not, you shall see the light of day again!" she told the forlorn sprig.

Feeling her way down a final step, the Pythia suddenly found herself again within the deepest room within the temple which she alone had the privilege to inhabit – the Adyton, the place of encounter between gods and men; some said it was the antechamber of Hades itself! Allowing her eyes to adjust to an even deeper darkness, she carefully placed the dish and laurel leaves upon a small shelf near where she stood, and in the soft light cast by the torch beyond the room, she made out the shape and lustre of the gilded cauldron at its centre.

She marvelled once again, as she always did, at the craftsmanship that had fashioned the smoothness of its burnished bronze surfaces, the sturdiness of its tri-wrought iron legs and the perfectly round and uniform holes that dotted the surface of the bowl of the cauldron, over which she ran the tips of her fingers, delighting her senses.

Taking hold of the thick folds of her robe, which kept her warm within the chill of the earth, she climbed with great effort into her cauldron seat, and reaching out for the dish of water and laurel leaves, she settled into place. She watched her bare feet dangling above the chasm beneath her seat, whose depths dropped away into the impenetrable darkness below.

With senses exquisitely tuned into this still and sombre space, she waited, her ears straining at the slightest sound, wondering what answer the great Apollo would give. Over and again her lips formed the question of the supplicant who eagerly awaited upon the surface of the earth for an answer, and gazing into the shallow dish she watched the reflection repeat back to her, her own words: "How are my children to live well, when I myself am dead?"

She shifted her gaze from the shallow dish to the chasm below and was seized with a terrible dread as the smell of the vapours became one with her own breath. The leaves shook in her trembling hand and her hair stood out like a sunburst around her face, now luminous, the colour of candle wax. She closed her eyes, yet rather than feeling comfort, she felt the terrifying sensation of falling into the abyss below. Fantastic shapes and figures loomed out of the darkness and made their ghostly way across her vision. *Surely*, she thought, *these are the attendants of Apollo himself!*

She cried out at the top of her voice for the whole of Hades to hear: "HOW ARE MY CHILDREN TO LIVE WELL, WHEN I MYSELF AM DEAD?" All at once her trembling ceased, followed by a great stillness of mind and body. She dismounted her tripod seat and poured the contents of the shallow dish into the cavernous void, an offering of thanks to the divine Apollo for giving answer to her question.

She wrapped the dish and laurel into the fold of her garment and made her way back up through the passage with a lightness in her step, overjoyed by the answer given. She repeated its contents over and over again, laughing at its alliterations and marvelling afresh at its wisdom.

The Pythia re-emerged at length, pushing open the curtain that divided the inner sanctum from that of the world without. There on the other side of the curtain stood waiting the high priest and her companion and at some distance, the trembling supplicant who dare not lift his eyes before the might of the Pythia, she who had the ear of Apollo himself!

Seeing him, the Pythia gave the dish and laurel to her companion in exchange for her head-covering. She approached the supplicant and cast her diaphanous veil about his head. Gazing at him with a look of infinite compassion, she proceeded to pronounce the oracle:

"The moral law renews itself in every generation,
  Where ever it blooms, there are no tombs,
Just joy and jubilation."

The high priest stood by and scribed the message on parchment before handing its contents to the supplicant, who with tears falling upon the marble floor, tucked the scroll into his breast. He bowed low to the one who had brought him god's favour and withdrew himself from the temple to live out his destiny.

The Pythia's companion dressed her in her purple robe and sandals and wrapped the protective veil about her head and shoulders, before leading her through the entrance of the temple and into the blinding light of the harsh noonday sun. Outside, throngs of pilgrims waited to catch sight of her, that they might receive a blessing from the deity.

As their cries went up, the Pythia drew her veil ever closer, overwhelmed by the sea of humanity which surged across the pavement, held back only by the temple guards brandishing their bronze shields and spears. The Pythia and her companion stepped into a litter and were carried by bearers down the pathway, ever further from the temple, whilst the priests offered counsel and blessings to the gathered throng.

The Pythia felt crushed by sudden fatigue. She rested her head heavily on the shoulder of her companion, whose silence over the last mile was balm to her soul. Reaching her dwelling by the woods, her companion helped her from the litter and to her door, while her guard took up his position nearby.

Murmuring thanks, she entered her home. The sprig of laurel was retrieved from under the fold of her garment and placed in the earthen vase by her window, that it might regain its vitality. Removing her veil and purple robe, setting them neatly aside, she donned a seamless linen tunic, ate a small supper and drank water from a pitcher to relieve her thirst. Then laying down upon her bed, she slept the length of two sunsets before rising in the stillness of the night to continue plying her fingers to the loom.

Glossary

Archetype: The original imprint of an innate and universal form rooted in psychological evolution.

Contemplative (Latin *con-templa-tio* – within the temple): Relating to the necessary dispositions of silence, focus and reflection in cultivating the pervasive and integrated awareness of the divine presence at the heart of all things.

Deep time: A perception of the unbroken thread of human becoming on whose psycho-evolutionary continuum each individual and generation sits, each one singularly and collectively adding to the lifting of consciousness from one generation to the next.

Depth psychology: A psychological framework that takes into account the more subtle and hidden aspects of a client's wellbeing, through the recognition of the interplay between the unconscious and conscious mind, whose therapeutic integration is approached from a position of health rather than pathology.

Existential emotions: Relating to the fundamental human perception of anxiety, anger and guilt experienced both personally and collectively as a result of psycho-evolutionary development.

Extrasensory perception (ESP): Awareness of information regarding events external to the self not gained through the senses or deduced by previous experience.

Liminal curtain (Latin *limen* – threshold): The demarcation between Pythian unconscious and conscious perception, which facilitates the movement between one aspect of consciousness and the other.

Liminal transparency: The degree of conscious awareness that a Pythian individual has in regards to the workings of their unconscious mind.

Linguistic recycling: A sudden special interest in a single word or phrase, using it in and out of context at will.

Metaphysics: A philosophy that explores the fundamental nature of reality and being.

Numinous: Of the mysterious, inexpressible personal encounter with the divine.

Oscillation: A movement between two points.

Prosody: The rhythm, speed, pitch and emphasis in patterns of speech.

Psyche: The combined processes of the unconscious and conscious mind whose individual and collective elements strive towards a state of equilibrium.

Psychic energy: The flow of energy between one's unconscious and conscious mind.

Psychic perception: A personal sensitivity to supernatural forces and influences.

Psycho-evolutionary: Pertaining to the evolutionary pressures that have shaped the formation of the human mind over millennia.

Psycho-relational: Pertaining to the psychological maturity gained over the course of one's life through necessary stages of relationship.

Psychotypical: The perception of life, particularly regarding the ease of facility in social and cultural bonding, experienced by the majority of the population as a consequence of a shared state of consciousness as default.

Pythia: The collective term for Pythian individuals.

Pythia of Delphi (8th century BC – 4th century AD): The title conferred upon any woman chosen to serve as high priestess throughout the history of the Temple of Apollo, in Delphi, ancient Greece.

Pythian: The term for an individual who identifies with the characteristics of Pythiism's theory of autism.

Pythiism (pronounced *pie-thi-ism*) (also known as autism): An alternative form of consciousness distinguished as an oscillation of psychic energy between the unconscious and conscious mind informing one's whole field of perception: cognitive, emotional, social, physical and spiritual.

Reflective Integration Therapy (RIT): The autism-specific therapeutic application of contemplative teachings and therapies designed to promote personal integration: body, mind and spirit, in a movement of ever-increasing health and wholeness, through the realisation of one's full personal potential.

Sticky consciousness: An altered self-perception regarding where one's body finishes and an object begins.

Subliminal: Operating below the threshold of consciousness.

Supernatural: Realms of existence and being that operate beyond the visible universe.

Surreal: Possessing a strange and dreamlike irrational quality.

Symbolic: Of words, objects, images, gestures or events that convey both personal and communal meaning.

Unconscious cognition: The methodical categorising and storing of information occurring below the level of conscious awareness.

Index